# TUTANKHAMUN'S
# CURSE

SOLVED

## I.L. COHEN

*Direct inquiries to:*

**NEW RESEARCH, LLC**
P.O. Box 29733
Elkins Park, PA 19027
or

*NewResearchLLC@gmail.com*


ISBN: 978-0-692-02020-3

**New Research, LLC**

# DEDICATION

This book, as well as all my other books,

is dedicated to

my

**MOTHER and FATHER**

who knowingly destroyed their lives,

their happiness, and their well-being

so as to build up mine.

I still have a big lump in my throat!

# ABOUT THE AUTHOR

I.L. COHEN was educated as an engineer. In the late 1970's he developed a keen interest in archaeology because it offered many challenging, unsolved problems. His earlier fieldwork at Stonehenge revealed an underlying basis for the solution of not only this enigmatic monument but also those of other equally-perplexing ancient civilizations.

The author spent the next 30+ years carrying out extensive research on Egyptian archaeology. His approach has been to evaluate archaeological remnants from an engineering, technological and scientific viewpoint. Through this approach, he was able to solve many outstanding mysteries of Egyptian archaeology.

He holds a Master's degree in Engineering from the University of Massachusetts-Lowell, is a Past-Vice President of the Archaeological Institute of America (LI), and has lectured widely on his research at various colleges and community associations.

The current book is part of a series that will reveal startling aspects of many of the enigmas found in archaeology and open a new door into understanding the history of mankind.

# ACKNOWLEDGEMENTS

First and foremost, I owe a special "thank you" to Dr. John Lundquist, the ex-director of the Oriental Division of the research section of the New York Public Library for his most efficient management ability and helpful assistance he extended to me during the 25 years of my research in his division. The cooperation extended to me by Dr. Lundquist, as well as by every single one of his assistant librarians, made it possible for me to continue my research activities in a most efficient manner. I thank all of them.

I also want to extend my appreciation to each and every page who worked very hard and efficiently to get for me—in a matter of 1 or 2 minutes—the hundreds of books and journals I required during said period.

At the same time, I want to register my thanks to each and every librarian of the Bryant Library (Roslyn, NY) for their most efficient and cheerful help they extended to me during the aforementioned 25 years period.

My thanks are also extended to Ms. Pamela Trush of Delaney-Designs for book design and layout, and to Ms. Heather Lee Shaw for illustrations and cover design.

In a broader sense, I—and all of us—are greatly thankful to all the archaeologists who labored under very, very hard conditions and sweltering heat to painstakingly excavate in Egypt for the past 200 years or so. They are the ones to whom we owe a great debt of appreciation for all the information they amassed and all the physical items they unearthed.

It is true that some of their interpretations do not seem to be correct today, in view of other aspects that modern science pointed out. Even so, past and present archaeologists are due a great degree of admiration and acknowledgement for the immense work they performed and the valuable information they submitted to the world of knowledge. Were it not for their toil and dedication we would not have had the possibility of analyzing the meanings of their findings in light of the advances made by modern science.

Every generation of researchers has at its disposal tools and scientific knowledge which earlier groups did not possess. While we consider that our more advanced interpretations are writing a new chapter in the history of humanity, we must not forget that we could not have reached that stage were it not for the immense work performed by previous and present generations of archaeologists and researchers.

They are the ones who created the first few rungs of a ladder of knowledge, so that I, and other researchers, got the possibility to step on these in order to reach the higher rungs of the same ladder. I am most thankful to them.

It has been reported that Newton was once asked how was it that he had seen further than others. His answer was the basis for the advancement of human knowledge. He replied: I saw further than others because I stood on top of their shoulders.

As a researcher in archaeology, I wish to thank past and present generations of archaeologists for the immense work they performed and are continuing to perform today. The results I obtained could not have been achieved were it not for them. I thank them all.

Finally, I owe a huge "Thank you" to every member of my family who constantly supported me during the long many years of my "digging" into the old records of archaeologists. But, the foremost expression of gratitude goes to my son, James, who devoted untold numbers of days and evenings to me and my work. Without him at my side, the present book would not have existed. My boundless gratitude and appreciation to you, Jim!

Yes, it is true what they say:

FACTS CAN BE STRANGER THAN FICTION

(Especially when reevaluating Egyptology)

# TUTANKHAMUN'S CURSE SOLVED

# INTRODUCTION

Ancient Egypt was considered to be an insoluble enigma. Many aspects discovered during 200 years of archaeological diggings did not make sense. Why was it necessary to create a heap of 7,100,000 tons of well-cut limestone blocks in order to build a burial place for a single human being—King Khufu?

Why were other Kings not honored in the same way?

Why was King Snofru entitled to have three sizeable pyramids named after him?

At his death, did they slice his body into three parts, placing each section in one of his so-called resting places? How could they do that when those three pyramids did not even contain any sarcophagi?

Did the ancient Egyptians enjoy themselves by lifting huge weights? In Khufu's pyramid, the burial chamber has 5 ceilings constructed out of 35 granite beams and 8 limestone beams, for a total weight of about 2,250 tons. Why?

Anyhow, why was it necessary to build 5 ceilings—a structural phenomenon not encountered in any other pyramid?

While such (and many more) rhetorical questions appear utterly silly—they are not. They are very realistic ones demanding proper, well-founded answers. It is my opinion that such unsolved mysteries could not have been handled properly during the past 200 years because the level of our general knowledge in science, technology, and engineering had not advanced to a point where answers could have been generated. However, with advancing knowledge we started to use our newly-acquired learning to solve old puzzles. Some of us, researchers, had now new tools which, if properly applied, could give us scientifically and technologically sound answers.

Through such a new approach I believe that I solved a number of the old enigmas which, in turn, threw a new light on other aspects of Egyptology. To some extent, it was a matter of one solution pointing to the answer of another unsolved problem.

Although I wrote a number of books (yet to be published), submitting solutions to many of our outstanding quandaries, I do recognize that this is only the beginning to a very large world of properly understood past history of humanity. It is hoped that upon realizing the foundation of my discoveries, research centers (such as Universities, Museums, etc.) will be interested in pursuing the leads I uncovered, and become active in promoting further research projects. Although the general areas have been located and partly solved, there is a vast area yet to be evaluated and calculated.

The future of these endeavors is exciting and promising for the new knowledge it will uncover.

When writing the present book, an intentional effort was made to include, as much as possible, the actual text of important statements and reports published by archaeologists. Naturally, it would have been easier and more concise to have paraphrased them and simply cite pages and publications that offered those passages. However, in view of the type of research project involved, the chosen approach has been considered to be more advantageous and important for the integrity of the extracted interpretation of that passage. Future researchers would then have it easier to reevaluate the data and possibly amend or fine-tune the conclusions reached in this book. In the final analysis, the interpretations offered in this study are based on scientific principles, as understood by this author. Yet, we know that science is a discipline with continuously widening horizons. As mankind's knowledge increases, additional scientific principles—or the interpretations of same—could also expand and undergo certain amendments. The next generation of science-oriented researchers might discover new meanings based on the same old data.

No footnotes have been included, nor notes at the end of each chapter of the book. Although such inclusions would have appeared more erudite, this author believes that diversionary "asides" greatly interrupt the ongoing cohesion and flow of the regular text. It becomes very disruptive to stop reading a given passage and leaf through pages in order to locate the proper notation at the end of the chapter or the book. Instead:

A - If the information to be imparted in the notation was meaningfully important, it is incorporated, within the text and made part of it.

B - If not, the page and year of the book of the quoted author was cited within the text itself. The bibliography includes all such publications of cited authors.

This book offers a number of pictures and line-drawings. The readers are urged to carefully study every one of them, spending a few minutes at each one as they are the essence of the evidence and explanations being offered in the text.

These pictures have not been included to embellish the presentation of the book. Instead, they are displaying the foundation of the various aspects discovered by this author and are part and parcel of the evidence submitted. As the old saying goes: "a picture is worth a thousand words." This is especially true in a book of this nature, one that submits newly discovered interpretations and evidences of age-old archaeological digs.

I am aware that, at various points in this book, I have provided what may appear to be an excessive number of quotations from various archaeologists. By doing so, I am trying to assist future researchers in locating more easily further information on the subjects at hand. While most readers will not need so many citations, professional researchers may find them helpful and time-saving for their own studies. I beg the indulgence of the readership.

CHAPTER ONE

# THE CURSE?

Tutankhamun was one of the least important, obscure kings of ancient Egypt, known to have occupied the throne for about 9 years only (ca 1358 to 1349 BC). He hardly can be considered to have ruled Egypt since he ascended the throne at age 9 and died at age 18, while governing power was concentrated in the hands of a regency. Some consider that the result of an autopsy performed early on, seems to have revealed that he died a violent death—from a blow to his head which, in turn, resulted in a brain clot. However, a CT-scan performed in February 2005 concluded that such was not the case. Others, using circuitous and contrived schemes, suggested that he had been murdered—an allegation without proof. In 1923, the discovery of his sealed tomb revealed extraordinary treasures.

This event constituted a very lucky break since most tombs of other pharaohs had been plundered before modern archaeologists got to them. Were it not for the fact that Tutankhamun happened to be the person buried in that particular tomb, he would have remained one of the forgotten kings of ancient Egypt.

His tomb was located at the end of a slanting trench dug into the side of a mountain, known as the Valley of the Kings, behind a well-concealed entrance—one that remained sealed for some 3,200 years. His burial site is referred to as KV62.

Two Englishmen, Howard Carter and Lord Carnarvon are credited with this discovery in 1922. On November 26,1922, these two gentlemen, along with the latter's daughter, Lady Evelyn, and Calender (Carter's assistant) were present when local laborers started to chisel

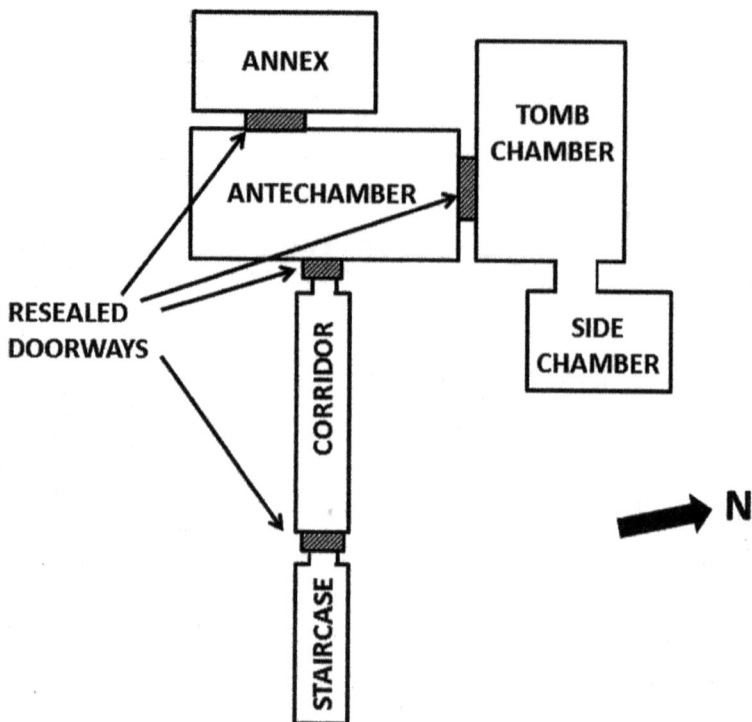

Fig. 1 *Layout of Tutankhamun's tomb (not to scale) © New Research, LLC*

into the stones sealing the second doorway—the one that would lead them to the so-called Antechamber of the tomb (Fig 1). They would discover that this room contained an enormous array of wealth, golden artifacts, and all sorts of furniture pieces. On February 17, 1923, they chiseled their way through the blocked doorways and entered into the main chamber that housed the golden sepulcher or, more specifically, the four nested, gold-plated wooden boxes that contained the stone sarcophagus and three mummy-formed golden coffins. The excitement of this find was universal. Both men, along with about twenty individuals, were present. Thereafter many other professionals and visitors, as well as a number of local laborers, spent hours within these chambers, inspecting, touching, and inventorying their contents.

This discovery stood out from all the other royal tombs located in the same Valley of the Kings area because of three important reasons:

1- The tomb was one of the very few burials that had been entered into once in the distant past but not really plundered during those intervening 3,200 years. Archaeologists had the possibility to study how the ancient Egyptians had proceeded to put a King to rest in his burial chamber.

2- The chambers contained a tremendous horde of valuables, golden artifacts. jewels. etc - constituting a most important find from the point of view of archaeology.

3- Soon after the discovery, this tomb was associated with what became known as the "Curse". A number of individuals died a short while after spending some time inside the chambers.

Fig. 2
*George Herbert,
5th Earl of Carnarvon,
at Howard Carter's
home on the Theban
west bank*

Why they died remained a mystery, as the medical profession of that time had been unable to pinpoint the exact causes. These mysterious deaths will be examined in the pages that follow.

A few weeks after this discovery, Lord Carnarvon fell ill and was taken to a room in a Cairo hotel. He ran a temperature of 104°F and shook with chills; these subsided the next day only to recur on the following day. This on-and-off condition continued for 12 days. "Every few days, one of his teeth chipped, or just fell out." (Hoving 1978, 221)

He was virtually unable to move while his neck-glands became swollen. On April 5, 1923 he died at the age of 57. The physician who attended to Carnarvon was at a loss to pinpoint the exact cause of death, except to observe a state of exhaustion. Some pointed out that Carnarvon had cut himself while shaving, creating a wound that became infected. Others had a different version. They contended that "... he was bitten by a mosquito. At first he thought nothing of it, but then the infection began to spread" (Leca 1981, 242).

In reality, none of them knew the real cause for an otherwise reasonably healthy man, age 57, to suddenly display most unusual and mysterious symptoms leading to death.

Another very similar case involved Arthur C. Mace, Carter's assistant, who was present at the opening of the tomb and had spent considerable time within its four walls.

Christopher C. Lee (1992) published an account of the life of this archaeologist. As a young man, Mace had been introduced to Egyptology by his cousin, the famous F. Petrie, whom he followed to Egypt and became his assistant during the late 1890s. He spent most of his time excavating tombs and other underground installations, located in various sites. Thereafter, and for a period of 5 years, he became assistant to Reisner, during which time he met Lythgoe, manager of the Department of Egyptian Art at the Metropolitan Museum of Art in New York City. Mace impressed Lythgoe and was invited to come to New York City and take over the position of Assistant Keeper at that

Museum. In due time, Mace returned to Egypt to work with Carter and was actively involved in breaking through the wall of Tutankhamun's burial chamber to inventory the contents.

Lee reported that, starting even before 1914, Mace's " ... health began to give cause for concern." During 1919 - 1920, he " ... still was not fit enough."

Although Mace was obviously not feeling well, no further specifics were given by Lee. By then, Mace had spent at least 15 years in Egypt, involved in opening various tombs and entering them.

After the opening of Tutankhamun's tomb in 1922-1923, the details of his health became clearer. By 1923, he was " ... looking increasingly thin and drawn, had to leave the laboratory to spend time in bed. His work stopped completely, his health now a serious problem." (Lee 1992,68). These generalities did not pinpoint the exact trouble until Lee gave us a very important clue:

> *"He easily gets tired."*
> *" ... his lack of energy frustrated him."*

This anemia continued steadily, until his death in 1928, at age 54.

The editors of the Journal of Egyptian Archaeology (v 15,1929, P 105-06) submitted Mace's life history in which they added a few pertinent details:

> *"After serving two winters on this task [i.e.working at Tutankhamun's tomb], Mace suffered a complete breakdown. The next four years were spent in England, on the Riviera, in Switzerland and in New York, in the attempt to recover his health, but in vain. He lost ground slowly but steadily, and finally died on April 6th, 1928. He made several attempts to work up his notes for the publication of the Amenemmes pyramid, and it was his bitter regret to find himself incapable of the energy required for the task."*

In brief, Mace suffered a continuously declining state of strength—a general anemia which his physicians were unable to remedy.

A third similar case concerned James Henry Breasted, a well-known and highly respected name in Egyptology. He was present at the opening of Tutankhamun's tomb after spending considerable time among ruins, temples, and tombs of ancient Egypt. As time passed, he started to suffer from high fever attacks, a condition that grew progressively worse. His son, Charles Breasted, wrote a book giving us some details about the health of his father, details that enhance the mystery when we compare symptoms with those of Carnarvon and Mace. He described it as follows:

> " ... But even before his arrival in Luxor he [his father] had begun to feel again the same feverish malaise he had experienced upon reaching London after his reconnaissance journey through the Near East in 1919-1920. This condition now grew worse. Each afternoon a fever returned to plague him with an aching throat and with alternate chills and periods when his blood burned in his veins and throbbed in his head. He assumed that he was suffering a recurrence of malaria acquired somewhere in Iraq, but the laboratory tests by the attending English physician failed to identify or quinine to allay the malady. The doctor ordered him to bed where he remained for more than six weeks throughout which with clocklike regularity the fever continued to return every noon and to recede in the early hours of the morning.

> He was permitted to get up only when Carter urgently required his presence at the tomb for consultations. On such occasions, with a linen mask over his mouth and nostrils to guard against dust,

*he would make the ten-mile round trip to The Valley in an open carriage... to return utterly exhausted and shaking with the fever.*

*... On November 21, 1935 from Genoa Harbor on his homeward voyage. In mid-Atlantic a sore throat he had acquired in Italy flared up with a high fever which he mistook for a recurrence of his old malaria, and which the Italian ship's doctor treated as such. When the ship reached New York he was desperately ill with what was found to be a virulent hemolytic streptococcic infection ..."* (Charles Breasted 1943, 357, 413)

Certain expressions used in these statements are thought-provoking. By the time Breasted reached Luxor in 1922 he was already experiencing a recurrence of *"... the same feverish malaise he had experienced .... in 1919 - 1920."* Each time he undertook a trip to the Valley of the King's area, Breasted returned *"... utterly exhausted and shaking with fever."*

These two statements refer again to "exhaustion" and "fever"—two symptoms that paralleled those of Canarvon and Mace. It is significant that the underlying cause was not malaria, a sickness that is accompanied by intermittent fever attacks. In 1922-23, English and Italian physicians were able to properly diagnose malaria and keep the disease under control. Yet, laboratory tests proved that it was not malaria nor did quinine have any effect. Ruling out malaria is very important since it requires us to seek out a different explanation. Breasted continued to display the same debilitating aspects for the rest of his life and died in December 1935, at age 70, of what physicians considered, at that time, to have been "a virulent hemolytic streptococcic."

The famous French archaeologist E. Chassinat (1903) wrote an obituary on the life of M. U. Bouriant, a past director of the Institut Francais d'Archeologie Orientale in Paris. He was born in 1849 and died in 1903, at the age of 54. Bouriant, was a French archaeologist who, in 1880, was attracted by Maspero (the Director General of the Department of Antiquities in Cairo) to come to Egypt where he spent a number of years, actively involved in digs. He is described as having been very active and vigorous, full of energy. However, starting in 1895, his health "declined perceptibly".

The "accumulated tiredness" of a "strenuous life" exerted an effect on him.

Upon his return from Egypt, in 1898, he was diagnosed as having hemiplegia. Chassinat specified:

> *"During almost five years, it became a daily struggle against fits of paralysis that were invading his body; there were alternating hopeful and deceptive periods. As was to be predicted, a powerful attack of apoplexy ended his life on June 19,1903"*
> (Translated from French text of Chassinat.)

If we read between the lines and replace Chassinet's words with more appropriate expressions, we promptly realize that Bouriant displayed the very same symptoms as those of Carnarvon, Mace, and Breasted. He, too, displayed exhaustion, tiredness, intermittent bouts with better and worse days, unable to move (fits of paralysis).

We are faced with another example of an individual, active in Egyptian archaeology who must have caught the same illness as displayed by the previously-mentioned three individuals. This case is important as Bouriant had never entered Tutankhamun's tomb, but was involved in other tombs while acting as an assistant to Maspero. This would indicate that other tombs, too, had been possessed by the "Curse."

There is a fifth archaeologist whose death might have been precipitated by contracting the same sickness. This example is being offered tentatively as the details of his health conditions are not sufficiently specific to be certain as to the character of his illness.

This individual is Bernard Grdseloff, who was born on July 1, 1915 and died October 8, 1950, at age of 35. An obituary was written by Ibrahim Harari (ASAE 1951 v51/1, 123) who depicted him as a very knowledgeable and greatly gifted archaeologist.

Among other details, Harari wrote:

*"At dawn of October 8, 1950, Bernard Grdseloff expired after a long and painful sickness that had kept him in bed during a long many years .... Although he was obliged to stay in bed due to his increasing weakness, he continued to be surrounded by his friends and colleagues. Such was the last condition of Grdseloff: - one of a man who was only a functioning brain, in touch with us through a most frail and exhausted body. One had difficulty to even recognize in him the young man of just a few years earlier ..."* (Translated from French text).

The condition of continuously increasing exhaustion and debilitating weakness does bring to mind one of the symptoms displayed by the previously cited cases. Until additional details of his condition are ascertained, we have to reserve judgment and consider Grdseloff as a potential — perhaps even probable — example of a victim of the "Curse."

The Service Des Antiquites De L'Egypte (Annales) published a small obituary notice (1951, 123) concerning archaeologist B. Grdseloff who had passed away at age 35, after "a painful sickness that had him bedridden for many years." We are not told the nature of his ailment.

As time went on, a number of published books reported that other individuals who had been present at Tutankhamun's tomb or who otherwise were involved in underground archaeological activities in Egypt, had died unexpectedly and under peculiar circumstances. All these reports, true or not, naturally created an aura of mystery, which engendered the superstitious belief that a powerful "Curse" or "Spell" had been instilled at Tutankhamun's tomb so as to protect it against intruders. Seemingly, the ancient Egyptian priests had used their magical, everlasting powers to punish anyone trying to disturb the peaceful rest of King Tutankhamun.

Various writers submitted examples of the "Curse", some of which are being quoted hereunder. It should be noted, however, that neither precise details of the circumstances of their deaths, nor the exact symptoms of their illnesses were specified. Medical reports issued in the 1920s and 1930s either drew a blank or were non-conclusive. As a result, direct inferences cannot be drawn at this stage of the research, except to take note of the death of a number of individuals involved in excavations of, or visits to, ancient Egyptian archaeological sites, as reported by other authors. Sixteen examples of these published incidents follow:

- While Breasted was bedridden and ailing in Egypt, a Canadian professor of literature, Mr. La Fleur, came to visit the tomb and was given a room directly alongside Breasted's chamber. After inspecting the tomb, La Fleur became desperately ill and died that very same night. The English physician who had been summoned thought that the cause was pneumonia. It is difficult to conceive that an otherwise healthy person can catch a cold or a germ and, within 24 - 48 hours, can die of pneumonia.

- The head of the Department of Egyptian Antiquities at the Louvre in Paris, Mr. Georges Benedite, was present at the tomb. After leaving the site, it is reported that he died suddenly and mysteriously. The local physicians diagnosed the cause to have been a stroke brought on by the overbearing heat (see CdE #1, 1925, pg 175).

- A friend of Lord Carnarvon, George Jay Gould (son of the famous American financier), upon hearing of the death of his friend, promptly traveled to Egypt. He was taken to visit the newly-discovered tomb. The next day, he was struck with a very high fever and that same evening, he died. Again, the local doctors were unable to diagnose the reason for this sudden death.

- Archibald Douglas Reed was the first radiologist to handle the mummy of Tutankhamun and took Xray pictures of the corpse. In 1924 he started suffering from debilitating attacks of intense weakness, and within a short time, he, too, died from "unexplained" causes.

- Likewise, Joel Woolf, an English industrialist, came to visit the tomb. It is reported that, on his way back to England, he died after running a very high fever.

- Georg Moller was in charge of the excavations of graves at Abu Sir and of the Theban City of the Dead, near Deir El Medine, spending a great amount of time inside tombs. At age 44 he suddenly died, ostensibly because of high fever and chills.

- Carter's assistant, Richard Bethall, died in 1929, supposedly of a circulatory collapse.

- The Director General of the Antiquities Department of the Egyptian Museum in Cairo, Dr. Gamal Mehrez, had spent a good part of his life in tombs and with mummies. At age 52, he collapsed and died. Officially his death was classified as circulatory collapse, the same diagnosis extended to others.

- Not every peculiar death occurred while entering Tutankhamun's tomb. For example, the famous Champollion who deciphered the Rosetta stone, had spent a number of years in Egypt, pursuing his archaeological interests. It is not known which ruins or temples he entered, nor what his state of health had been. We do know, however, that upon his return to France in 1832 he had "paralytic seizures" and died at the age of 42.

- Winstone (1986, 119) reported that the assistant to Champollion, an artist named Nestor d' Hôte, met a peculiar death:

  *"Nestor had made countless drawings and notes of the Valley of Kings where he and his companions resided in the tomb of one of the Ramesses. The death of Champollion in 1832, following a terrible fit of apoplexy, caused Nestor to make a nostalgic pilgrimage in the path of his master in 1838 ... Nestor died on the Red Sea coast in 1842, at the age of 38, exhausted by his work ..."*

The fact that a 38 year old man died of "exhaustion" engenders the question as to what extraordinary type of strenuous activity could have been involved.

Although such a serious and fatal exhaustion is a recurring symptom among the afflicted victims, we can, of course, not jump to the conclusion that Nestor d'Hôte, who set up residence in an underground tomb, had been exposed to the effect of the "Curse." The data on hand is not sufficient to provide the proper foundation for such a conclusion. It is thought-provoking, but not conclusive. Further research is necessary.

- Another important archaeologist who spent years in Egypt was Giovanni Battista Belzoni. He discovered the grave of Seti I where he spent an entire year copying murals found in those subterranean chambers. At a later date he discovered the entrance to Khafre's pyramid in Gizeh and entered its passages and burial room. In 1823, while traveling in Africa, he suddenly fell prey to the same illness that attacked future archaeologists: very high fever and raving delusions, confused speech, and chills. Within a few days, he died at the age of 45. Had he been a victim of the effect of the Curse? Perhaps, yet we are not certain until further details of his health conditions become known.

- Dr. Bilharz, a German physician, took great interest in performing autopsies on mummies. In 1862 he guided a group of German dignitaries to see various tombs. On his way back, Bilharz suffered attacks of very high fever and paralysis. After spending two weeks in a coma, he died at age 37, without regaining consciousness. His doctor friends were unable to pinpoint the cause for his mysterious death.

- A few years later, in 1858, the same fate befell four European tourists who had just visited the pyramids and the tombs in the Valley of the Kings. They all died suddenly from unknown causes, even though local authorities registered their deaths as being attributable to the plague, pneumonia, etc.

- Other Egyptologists displayed different symptoms: attacks on their nervous systems. Carter did not display the same negative physical reactions as some of the others. He continued to live for another 16 years but was constantly plagued by deep emotional depression. He also suffered from an incurable glandular disorder (Brunton 1939, 53).

- Carter's friend, Dr. E.White, had participated in the opening of the tombs; he, too, suffered great nervous depression, hindering normal activities on a great many days.

- The father of Richard Bethell—Carter's secretary— spent time in Egypt, sharing some of the archaeological activities of his son. He, too, experienced fits of depression which ultimately led him to commit suicide by jumping out of a window.

It should be noted, however, others that were present at the opening of Tutankhamun's tomb, survived for a number of years, seemingly without ill effects, although their state of health is not known. They included well-known archaeologists such as Gardiner, Engelbach, Lythgoe, Lacau, and Burton. It has been reported that thirteen of the original twenty-two individuals present at the penetration of Tutankhamun's chamber died within a relatively short time thereafter, under circumstances that could not be described as normal. We do not know the fate of the Egyptian laborers, nor of the hundreds of early visitors who entered the tomb.

Most of these deaths had been cited by Leca (1981, 241 - 246) and Vandenberg (1975).

Another author, Brackman (1976, 162 - 164) submitted some additional names of individuals who might have been subjected to the "Curse", to wit:

- M. Cassanova, of the College de France, who had been involved in excavations of tombs, "died unexpectedly" (Not a very illuminating description.)

- Colonel Aubrey Herbert, Lord Carnarvon's half-brother, had been present at the opening of the sarcophagus of Tutankhamun. He is reported to have died during an attack of "temporary insanity" (whatever this term might mean).

- Dr. Jonathan W. Carver, one of Carter's assistants, seems to have met an unusual death. We are hardly given any details of the type of death involved, but are expected to believe that he too had been a victim of the same mysterious ailment.

- Lady Elizabeth Carnarvon seems to have died of an "insect bite", another unlikely cause similar to the one cited in the case of Lord Carnarvon.

The well-known archaeologist, L. Habachi (1956, 43 - 46) pointed out that five Egyptian egyptologists had died suddenly within a span of three months during 1949, namely:

Darwish Khalid (known for discovering the two colossi of Amenophis III),

Abd El-Salam Mohamed, (active in Saqqara and Dahshur)

Mohamed Abd El-Moneim Yousef (archaeologist and photographer),

Mina Riskallah, (Director of the Coptic Museum),

Rizkallah N. Makramallah (archaeologist)

As no details of symptoms nor their health conditions were given, such citations cannot be helpful in evaluating the real reason for their deaths, except in the case of Makramallah, who was said to have been suffering from a heart condition.

When evaluating the various deaths that have been reported on a consistent basis, it is important not to jump to the conclusion that all had died from the "Curse". Unfortunately, when the rumor mill started propagating this subject, it generated a life of its own with additional embellishments. For example, Vandenberg (1975, 27) reported that Mace died, seemingly in 1923, describing his death as follows:

> *"The American archaeologist Arthur Mace, who had been asked by Carter to help open the tomb and who had ripped out the last chunk of wall blocking the entry to the main chamber, complained about growing exhaustion after Carnarvon's death. Finally, he fell into a deep coma that doctors were unable to diagnose and died in the same hotel as had Lord Carnarvon."*

This information does not correspond to the real facts. Mace did not die in the same hotel as Carnarvon. In fact, he did not even die in Egypt; what's more, he did not die in 1923, but on April 6th, 1928, as reported by C.C.Lee (1992) and by the editors of the *Journal* of *Egyptian Archaeology* (v 15,1929, P 105-106). He died in Haywards Heath, Sussex, England (Dawson & Uphill 1995, 267).

Likewise, Leca (1981, 243-244) wrote on the same subject, but was equally in error when reporting that:

> *"Then in 1926 Georges Benedite "... perished of pneumonia...followed shortly by Arthur C. Mace."*

This passage implies that Mace died in 1926, or perhaps in early 1927—which, again does not correspond to the facts.

These inaccuracies are not the fault of the cited authors who probably picked up the information from the oft-repeated and embellished rumors that, with time, became "facts."

We have to be very careful to properly double-check our data, reverting, as much as possible, to independent and verifiable sources. It is quite possible that many of the cited people died from the same cause. However, before they get included in the list of victims, a thorough search of their symptoms has to be made, along with their precise activities and circumstances surrounding their deaths.

Based on an overview of the various deaths that occurred among individuals involved in entering pyramids, tombs and temples, we observe a repeating pattern. Two main classes of symptoms seem to reoccur:

1) Great fatigue, exhaustion, depression, circulatory collapse, strokes.

2) Very high fever, intermittent chills, swollen glands, some nervous disorders.

When we compare these factors to known symptoms quoted in modern medical diagnostic records, we discover that these conditions exist among people who were exposed to radioactivity.

We learned about these conditions only after the atomic explosions at Hiroshima, Nagasaki, the subsequent experimental test performed in the Pacific Islands, and from the Chernobyl powerplant fall-out accident. This new information, gathered since 1945, was unknown to the physicians in 1923 at a time when Tutankhamun's tomb was entered into.

Radiation sickness was clearly described by Brodine (1974, 58):

### High Doses of Radiation

*When radiation doses reach hundreds of rads, the body's recuperative capabilities are overwhelmed. The short-term whole body dose that would kill half of a group of healthy adults is estimated at 400-500 rads, and few people would be expected to survive doses above 700 rads.*

*Exposure to more than 200 rads to the whole body, as in nuclear war or in a nuclear accident, produces acute radiation sickness. For the first couple of hours after exposure there is no burn, no sore, no aching; then a severe malaise begins. The exposed individual feels weak and sick, loses his appetite, and is soon nauseated and vomiting. Headache, dizziness, and even prostration may appear. This acute upset increases in intensity, reaches a peak in hours, and is completely over in one to three days. For two to three weeks, the subject feels well and considers himself spared. But during this latent period, telltale changes in the blood can be easily detected by appropriate tests. Perhaps a matter of hours after exposure the lymphocytes fall to low levels, followed by the other white blood cells (neutrophils), and later by the platelets and red cells. In the third week, the patient feels that he is suddenly coming down with an acute infectious disease. Chills, fever, fatigue, and shortness of breath occur; the hair on the body and head starts to fallout. Within a day or two, he is sick enough to be hospitalized. Now the bone marrow depression and blood abnormalities announce themselves in skin hemorrhages, nose and gum bleeding, and bloody diarrhea. Infection, especially in the mouth, is often a complication.*

*This is the picture of acute radiation sickness after exposure of the whole body to 200-400 rads. Everyone exposed to this dose requires medical care, but over half survive. Some of those who recover may experience somatic effects months or years later. With smaller doses of radiation, the initial sickness is milder and the only late symptom may be fatigue, although changes in the blood can occur. With larger doses of 500-600 rads, the initial sickness is longer and more intense, the latent period is shorter or absent, and the outcome depends more on gastrointestinal damage and bloody diarrhea than on blood changes or infection.*

*When the radiation is delivered to only a portion of the body, much higher exposures can be tolerated. If radiation is delivered over a long period of time or if the dose is not high enough to cause radiation sickness or death, it can have less dramatic but nevertheless serious consequences that may not become apparent for years or that may be discernible only statistically in the increase in incidence of some particular disease among people exposed to radiation or in the increase in incidence of genetic defects in their descendants.*

A classification of symptoms pertaining to radiation sickness has been published in the 40th edition of *Current Medical Diagnosis and Treatment* (2001, 1551-2) which submits the following highlights:

> *A- HEMATOPOIETIC TISSUES; Injury to the bone marrow may cause diminished production of blood elements ... Damage to the blood forming organs may vary from transient depression of one or more blood elements to complete destruction.*
>
> *B- CARDIOVASCULAR SYSTEM: Pericarditis with effusion or constrictive pericarditis may occur after a period of months or even years....*
>
> *C- RESPIRATORY TRACT: High or repeated moderate doses of radiation may cause pneumonitis, often delayed for weeks or months.*
>
> *D- MOUTH, PHARYNX, ESOPHAGUS, AND STOMACH: Mucositis with edema and painful swallowing of food may occur within hours or days after onset of irradiation. Gastric secretion may be temporarily (occasionally permanently) inhibited by moderately high doses of radiation.*
>
> *E- INTESTINES; Inflammation and ulceration may follow moderately large doses of radiation.*
>
> *F- ENDOCRINE GLANDS AND VISCERA: Hepatitis and nephritis may be delayed effects of therapeutic radiation. The normal thyroid, pituitary, pancreas, adrenals, and bladders are relatively resistant to low or moderate doses of radiation....*
>
> *G- NERVOUS SYSTEM: The brain and spinal cord are much more sensitive to acute exposures than the peripheral nerves.*

*H- RADIATION SICKNESS—SYSTEMIC REACTION:*
*Anorexia, nausea, vomiting, weakness, exhaustion,*
*lassitude, and in some cases prostration may occur,*
*singly or in combination. Dehydration, anemia and*
*infection may follow.*

The individuals described here displayed many of these symptoms, singly or in combination. The same publication offered additional explanations about the immediate causes of death after a serious exposure to radiation:

> "*Death after acute lethal radiation exposure is usually due to hematopoietic failure, gastrointestinal mucosal damage, central nervous system damage, widespread vascular injury, or secondary infection. The acute radiation syndrome may be dominated by central nervous system, gastrointestinal, or hematologic manifestations depending on dose and survival. Four hundred to 600 cGy of x-ray or gamma radiation applied to the entire body at one time may be fatal within 60 days; death is usually due to hemorrhage, anemia, and infection secondary to hematopoietic injury. Levels of 1000 - 3000 cGy to the entire body destroy gastrointestinal mucosa; this leads to toxemia and death within 2 weeks. Total body doses above 3000 cGy cause widespread vascular damage, cerebral anoxia, hypotensive shock, and death within 48 hours.*"

[For reference: 1 cGy = 1 rad = 1-20 rem (varies with type)]

Central nervous system damage, secondary infection, and anemia were cited as some of the outstanding causes of death from radiation. Each one of these symptoms was encountered among the Egyptologists under discussion.

A great many detailed studies have been performed to determine the effects of various doses radiation on the human body. Roxburgh (1987, table 1.15) submitted the following general overview:

| Dose (rems) | Effects |
| --- | --- |
| 0 - 25 | A dose around 25 rem may reduce the white blood cell count. |
| 25 - 100 | Nausea for about half those exposed, fatigue, changes to blood. |
| 100 - 200 | Nausea, vomiting, fatigue, death possible, susceptible to infection (low white blood cell count). |
| 200 - 400 | A lethal dose for 50 of those exposed especially in absence of treatment. Bone marrow, spleen (blood-forming organs) damaged. |
| Over 600 | Fatal, probably even with treatment. |

The information underlines a very important after-effect: the change in the white blood cell count which reduces the proper functioning of the immune system, as a result of which, infections are easily developed. This indicates that Carnarvon must have been exposed to over 100 rem radiation. We now have an explanation why so many Egyptologists and physicians were misguided when evaluating his death: they had no idea of the very existence of radiation sickness.

It must be pointed out that not everybody present at the opening of the tomb died in the same manner. Some continued to live long after the incident of 1923. This, too, is part of the characteristics of radiation sickness, as ably described by Brodine.

To sum up: Radiation can affect people in different ways. There are a great many factors that determine that person's degree of sickness or his/her recuperative capacity to exposure to radiation. For example: amount of radiation, exposure time, part of the body that had been exposed, whether single or multiple exposures with cumulative effects were involved, original health condition of victim, etc.

It is very significant to observe that the individuals who died "mysteriously" while being active in underground archaeology in Egypt, displayed a few or most of the symptoms described above.

Of course, in 1923, and for many years thereafter, the medical profession had no knowledge of the entire subject and could not possibly have diagnosed correctly a case of radiation sickness. In fact, the very existence of radiation in ancient Egypt, would have been the furthest concept entering into the minds of Egyptologists or anybody else. As a result, anything whose cause was unknown, became a "mystery", and for ignorant or superstitious societies, it became a "curse."

Unfortunately for them, there is no such a thing as a "curse". A sickness, no matter how peculiar, has a physical origin. The fact that we might not be able to diagnose the exact pathological cause at a given time, is not a reason to invent the alibi of the "curse". More realistically evaluated, it should have been assigned to our ignorance at the time of its occurrence. It is true that quite a few archaeologists who were involved with Tutankhamun's tomb or with other underground digs in Egypt, seemed to have met peculiar deaths. Even so, a positive and direct correlation cannot be established unless their bodies were to be exhumed and tests performed. Statistically, there is a meaningful accumulation of incidents which should alert us to a peculiar set of circumstances; nevertheless, a direct and exact conclusion cannot be drawn at this point in time.

However, in the cases of Carnarvon, Mace, Breasted, and Bouriant, we face a much more positive situation: their health conditions and symptoms were clearly established and reported. These anomalies displayed during the last few years of their lives concord with the unique types of symptoms experienced by individuals exposed to dosages of radiation, as described by Brodine.

One is inclined to conclude that the aforementioned four archaeologists had been victims of radiation sickness. They must have absorbed moderate to high doses of radiation on a cumulative basis. The fact that all four were felled by the sickness described above is enough to conclude that Tutankhamun's chambers (as well as other tombs), contained radioactive substances or lingering radioactivity within their four walls. We do not necessarily need statistical support from the deaths of others to convince ourselves that these four individuals had been irradiated. Because of their peculiar deaths, the reason for the demise of the other individuals becomes more meaningful and probable. Nevertheless, a detailed investigation should be undertaken to establish the conditions of health and symptoms displayed by each of the other victims cited earlier.

# WHAT ABOUT
# HOWARD CARTER?

Carter did not start his adult activities as a professional archaeologist. In fact, originally, he hardly knew anything about this subject. He was born in England in May 1874, received a regular primary and secondary education, while developing a very good skill in drawing and painting, but not for academic subjects. In Oct. 1891, at age of only 17½ he was hired by the Egypt Exploration Fund as a draftsman and sent to Egypt to serve and assist the archaeo-

Fig. 3   *Howard Carter, 1924*

logical activities of Petrie and Newberry. He proved himself quite capable, and with time, advanced through different assignments until he was put in charge of specific digs. In 1922, he, along with Carnarvon, discovered the untouched tomb of Tutankhamun. And, as the saying goes: the rest is History.

Carter continued to be active for a number of additional years in Egyptian archaeology, until he died in England on March 2, 1939, at age 65.

T.G.H. James published an excellent book (1992), submitting a very detailed history of the events in Carter's life.

We are facing an important quandary. It is well-known that a number of archaeologists and visitors to the tomb of Tutankhamun died mysterious, early deaths. The previous chapter has displayed some of the detailed symptoms of four victims who had died unexpectedly with symptoms consistent with the effects of radiation sickness. While a great many other individuals had been reported as having been felled by the "Curse", no solid details of their symptoms were forthcoming. As a result, these unproven cases had to be put aside until bona-fide details could be established. However, the four examples pinpointed displayed a common trait: they all were involved as digging archaeologists of tombs or constant visitors to ancient Egyptian tombs. Although they all fell very sick, physicians in charge could not understand the cause.

Carter was one of the people who devoted his entire life in and around such tombs. While he had been active in many tombs before 1922, he spent an inordinate amount of time in Tutankhamun's burial chambers after said date. Yet, he lived for some additional 17 years or so after the 1922 discovery of KV62, before dying at age 65. Many analysts pointed out and underlined this fact, so as to prove that the premature death of some of the others could have been simply a fluke, a haphazard happening, disconnected from any outside influence or events.

The present research has submitted the underlying cause for the deaths of those whose conditions could be verified, based on established facts. Their deaths were not a simple matter of haphazard chance.

If radioactivity was present in Tutankhamun's tomb, why was Carter not felled, the same way as the others, especially as he was the one who spent so much time inhaling its atmosphere and exposing his body to the mummy and the artifacts?

In first place, and as stated earlier, our medical records confirm that every person reacts differently when exposed to radiation. And, in second place, are we certain that Carter's health had not been impaired? Are we sure that he had not suffered from unexplained ill health?

Unfortunately, the vast majority of published articles, reports, and books hardly allude to Carter's health. However a book written by James (1992) gives us certain details of Carter's life that should raise doubts in our minds. The salient passages direct us to a new understanding of Carter's health and alert us to the fact that something unusual was happening to him.

James' interspersed remarks start with conditions observe in 1905-that means 17 years before the discovery of the KV62 tomb:

*"His naturally depressed nature was never enlivened by the kinds of enthusiastic behaviour which would have been proper for someone in his early thirties ..."* *(121)*

*"Later in the summer he was to fall ill again. The nature of the illness is not made clear in a letter Maspero wrote to him on 8 October; but Carter's superior was concerned enough to comment..."* *(121)*

Even as early as 1905, we encounter a youngish man, 31 years old, who had spent 14 years in and around ancient Egyptian tombs and who displayed some health problem, as well as depression and/or nervous disorders.

Colleagues of his, such as the archaeologist Maspero, who noticed and referred to his ill health, were unable to specify and name his sickness. They only knew that he was constantly "sick". These important observations should be kept in mind, as we continue to note the comments about Carter's health expressed by people who realized that something was wrong without being able to specify the malady involved.

In 1923, about one week after the opening of the tomb, Lady Evelyn, daughter of Carnarvon, wrote a note to Carter, in which she stated:

> *"I am so terribly sorry to hear that you have taken seedy with your tummy out of order. I wish I had been there with you to look after you dear—for you know how I fancy myself at nursing!" (255).*

Here, she refers to the "seedy tummy" problem of Carter—whatever that might have meant. Again, we note a friend referring to his sickness without being able to specify what the sickness is (obviously, because she did not know what was involved). Nevertheless, we become aware that Carter seems to suffer from some sort of problem located in his lower body. This hint will become clearer when we read some words used in Carter's official death certificate.

Carnarvon died on April 5, 1923 in Cairo. Carter had gone there to be present during the final days of his friend:

> *"When he returned to Luxor on 16 April Mace noted that he was 'looking rather tired and washed out'"* (259)

James reported that in early 1926:

> *"The strain which Winlock noted had threatened to upset the new and welcome equanimity displayed by Carter during the 1925-6 season led to a deterioration in his health in the New Year. In February he decided to run up to Aswan for a rest. Breasted remarked in a letter to his son Charles that 'He is in very bad health'"(351).*

Again and again, we are being told of a "deterioration in his health" without being given any hints or specific details. With hindsight, we now realize that none of the individuals around Carter knew the nature of his illness.

For that matter, neither did Carter. Otherwise, he would have told his friends what disorder was involved. This also means that all the doctors that were supposed to cure his illness were at a loss to understand the baffling problem they were facing. As a result, his friends could only notice Carter's debilitating condition. All they could verbalize was: "Carter is in very bad health."

In the 1927-28 season, Carter, who had arranged to ship some of Tutankhamun's artifacts to Cairo, traveled to that city. In his book, James (p 366) pointed out that

> *"He was not particularly well at the time—indeed he was rarely in a state of good health for the rest of his life ... It was not surprising that his patience was at times stretched..."*

We witness a repeat of previous observations: Carter was very sick. Everybody was aware of it. Nobody was able to pinpoint the cause for his constant debilitating health condition nor for his nervous disorders. As time went on, the same refrain continued to be repeated by James:

> . " *... the 1928-29 season, ... the problems of the illness-ridden time were nothinq compared with the exasperation of the 1929-30 season"* (373).

Mrs Mace reported to her Mother:

> *"Mr Carter was coming over; he arrived looking desperately ill."* (pg 292)

Again, with the passing of time, Carter was not getting any better. His mysterious "sickness" continued and even became worse. James reported that the situation in the 1930's had not improved:

> "... he was just destitute of spirit, and a seriously ill person. Throughout his life he suffered from indifferent health, and, as has been suggested earlier, many of his moods were surely the result of feeling miserably sick...

> " ...His condition deteriorated seriously from the mid-1930s, the trouble being a glandular affliction which would be diagnosed as Hodgkin's disease."

For the first time in his presentation James refers to a specific illness. At least, at this late period in his life, do we now get an inkling of the problem that is emerging, that is what some doctors thought they understood. However, in this regard, reading an excerpt from a letter Carter wrote to a friend is informative:

> "I did not leave London until the second week in December. In November my ills took a turn for the bad, but happily I found an excellent doctor who seemed to understand my trouble. He dosed me with arsenic and gave me deep-ray (a form of X-ray) and in the course of a month I became another being. The misfortune was that the ray treatment brought on a temporary form of acute nausea and loss of the sense of taste, which was certainly a bore ...." (395)

These few lines of Carter give us a very clear picture. During all the elapsed years, doctors had not been able remotely to diagnose his illness. This was very understandable because of the lack of medical knowledge in those years, a repeat of the situation that had faced Carnarvon. At least, this last "excellent" physician thought that he could diagnose the problem and attempted some sort of a cure, albeit with side-effects.

James gave us the final episode in Carter's health saga and death:

*"The progress of his life, made increasingly burdensome by illness, passed into a steady decline in his last years, which brought him by early 1939 to a condition which required a nurse in attendance.*

*She kept a general eye on his condition and on the attention he received, but there was little that could be done to prevent the inevitable end. His death certificate gives two causes of death, cardiac failure and lymphadenoma, the former being the immediate cause, and the latter the effective cause. Carter's condition would now be described as malignant lymphoma, or, less technically, Hodgkin's disease. It is marked by an enlargement of the lymphatic tissues and spleen, and considered to be a cancerous condition. For Howard Carter it was surely a seriously debilitating condition, leading to a painful and miserable death..." (406)*

The Wikipedia Encyclopedia describes:

*"Lymphoma is a cancer that begins in the lymphocytes of the immune system. There are many types of lymphomas and in turn lymphomas are a part of the broad group of diseases called hematological neoplasms."*

We now know the cause of his illness: destruction of the immune system, blood system, and cancer are the characteristic symptoms of radiation sickness.

Carter had been exposed to radiation which had killed him.

Some critics could argue that people who die from disorders of the immune system, or lymphoma, or hematological diseases, or who display some impairment to the nervous system, were not necessarily exposed to radioactivity, as a number of these health problems could have arisen independently.

That is true. However, in the present case, we have to take into account the confluence of the various aspects that were present around the felled individuals, factors that clearly underline the reality of the existence of radioactivity surrounding these victims, including Howard Carter.

*Howard Carter (kneeling) and assistants opening the shrine doors
in the tomb's burial chamber (NY Times photo archive)*

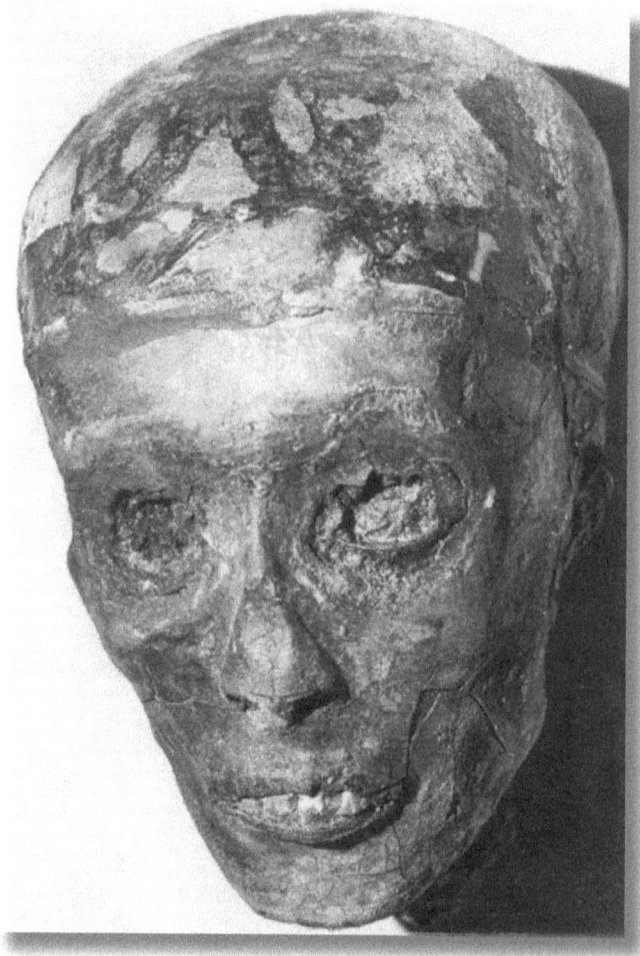

Fig. 4  *Blackened head of Tutankhamun*

CHAPTER TWO

# THE CORPSE

There is another very peculiar aspect that tends to support the conclusion arrived at by the present research project. The mummified body of the boy-king was found inside several nested gold-plated wooden caskets which, in turn, contained one stone and three gold sarcophagi. The body was taken to a laboratory where it was unwrapped. An autopsy was performed. To the surprise of everybody, the following facts were observed:

1- The King's face, and other parts of his body, displayed several burnt and blackened spots as though he had been exposed to flames or very high searing heat (Fig. 4).

2- His hair had fallen off. It is very doubtful that they shaved his hair before burial, as this was not the practice of the ancient Egyptians. In fact, the mummies of some of the other Kings, also buried in the Valley of the Kings, had full sets of hair, while others did not. The mummies of Thutmosis II, Thutmosis IV, Ramses V, Ahmosis I, Septah, and Ramses II displayed hair. However, Thutmosis I, Ramses VI, Amenophis III, Merneptah, and Seti I were found to be hairless.

3- Carter (1972, 157) made the following additional observation:

*"...I should mention that the charred remains of the mummy itself show no traces of the cause or causes of the young King's death..."*

A "charred" remain denotes an object that has been exposed to very high heat or flames. Such a condition would be in line with the expectation for a person exposed to radiation or hit by a powerful bolt of lightning. It naturally raises the question whether the entire body had been exposed to radiation or whether only specific parts of the body were involved.

In his book, Reeves (1990, 113) showed a picture of "Tutankhamun's blackened left hand..." Unless the hand had been painted black, which is doubtful, we might conclude that it too had been exposed to a powerful dose of radiation.

Douglas E. Derry undertook the job of unwrapping this mummy. He encountered great difficulty in doing so because of the conditions prevailing, which he described as follows:

> "... the bandages were in a state of extreme fragility and crumbled at a touch. This seems to have been due to the inclusion of some humidity at the time of interment, as well as the decomposition of the unguents, which generated a high temperature and thus brought about a sort of spontaneous combustion which carbonized the wrappings. This has frequently been observed and has given rise to the idea that mummies so affected have been burnt ... the increasing state of disintegration of the wrappings was noticeable. These in many places were reduced to dust, and in no case could any length of bandage or sheet be removed intact." (Derry 1972, 226)

Derry found the bandages had been "carbonized". This is an important observation and key to the solution of the enigma. Carbonization occurs when vegetable matter is exposed to very high heat in the absence of air. The lack of oxygen impedes proper normal combustion, accompanied by flames. The best example is wood which, under those conditions, would have ended up as charcoal, a situation constantly encountered in many of the earlier tombs. Cotton or linen bandages, being less compact and more delicate than wood, would carbonize and naturally fall apart when touched. It is not the "decomposition of the unguent" that created very high temperatures on the body of the King. If that were the case, all the other mummies that had been unbundled should have displayed the same conditions. And yet, a great many of them did not; instead, archaeologists were able to unwrap them and end up with long lengths of bandages, despite the fact that all contained unguent. The concept of attributing this condition to spontaneous combustion is misplaced. Of course, Derry cannot be blamed for his misinformation; during his time, no one knew what radiation meant and what its aftereffects were. In fact, even Mace was perplexed. In his diary, he entered the following remarks on April 5, 1923:

> *"Puzzle why some linen perishes while other actually touching it does not. Must be a question of original quality of the thread work."*

We must not be surprised at this unscientific determination made by Mace. In 1923 there was no possibility for him (or anybody else) to have known the effect of the intensive waves of heat a radioactive substance would have created.

The disintegration of linen gives us a very important clue. We can now determine which tombs had contained radioactive materials and which did not. Mummies with satisfactory bandages had been placed in tombs that had not been used as storage sites for radioactive substances. Mummies with "crumbling" bandages had been exposed to searing heat whose source was the effect of radiation.

If Tutankhamun's body, either before, during, or after mummification had been exposed to radiation, such a condition could have created very elevated levels of heat, enough to burn him and carbonize the delicate gauze-like bandages. In fact, his chambers had originally contained enough radioactive materials for their lingering effects to have been felt by modern-time archaeologists.

It should also be pointed out that Tutankhamun's head was no longer connected to the spine because it had been severed. We are not certain whether this decapitation occurred while Carter was trying to extricate the skeleton from the casket to which it was glued due to the hardened unguent that seem to have been poured over it. It possibly might have happened when Derry tried to unwrap the mummy. A third alternative possibility exists. The corpse was already damaged before it had been placed in his sarcophagi.

Such a thought cannot be considered improbable as the body of King Seti I, when found, proved to have been "decapitated" too. What's more, let us remember that Seti I's mummy displayed the same conditions as those of Tutankhamun. He, too, had a blackened, "burnt"-type skin, and also had lost his hair. Such surprising similarities induce us to conclude that, in all probabilities, Seti I's tomb had been used to store radioactive substances, while he had been exposed to radiation before or after his death. This parallelism implies that other mummies had probably been irradiated during their lifetime.

It is interesting to observe that in the Annex room of Tutankhamun's tomb, they found a gold-plated wooden scepter with an inscription that read;

*"The Beautiful God, beloved, dazzling of face like Aten when it shines." (Carter 1972, 210)*

Aten being the sun, it meant that the King's face was "shining". In modern terminology, we might call it luminescence. The Egyptians very correctly described what they saw: a glowing or shining face. The significance of this observation remains to be elucidated.

If Tutankhamun's site contained such lethal substances, then it is logical to assume that other underground tombs must have stored them too. We have indirect confirmation of such a situation through the statements of Lee and Breasted.

Lee told us that even before 1914 Mace's "... health began to give cause for concern ..." And that by 1919-20 he "... still was not fit enough." This means that before 1922-23, when Tutankhamun's tomb was discovered and entered into, Mace had already been exposed to radiation, even before 1914!

The same goes for Breasted. His son reported that, before reaching Luxor, Breasted displayed "... the same feverish malaise ... which he had experienced since 1919-20." This indicates that Breasted, too, had been exposed to radiation prior to his activities within the newly discovered tomb of Tutankhamun.

The present study points out the importance of re-analyzing the whole gamut of ancient Egyptian archaeology, to determine whether other aspects of that society were involved in this most unexpected facet, a scientific understanding that our modern era discovered only some 95 years ago. When such a task is performed, we will probably find that many unsolved mysteries in Egyptology become much clearer and offer cogent explanations and solutions.

Desroche-Noblecourt (1963, 224) summarized the mystery to be solved:

> *"Some day it may become clear why Tutankhamen's head was prepared in a totally different manner from those of most of the other sovereigns found in the cashe of Deir el Bahar ... Those other great Kings of Egypt still have almost living heads of hair..."*

Perhaps that "someday" might be at hand, since we now understand how radiation displays its effects.

Although radiation seems to have played a part in this King's condition, there is an additional reason that might have contributed to his death, namely: electrocution. Normally, such a thought would have been considered outrageously illusionary, yet, when we carefully evaluate some aspects shown on ancient Egyptian murals, we must conclude that said society had electric power. To be sure, the general public, most of the priestly class, and even royalty, did not have the slightest understanding of what was involved.

Various aspects encountered in their archaeology, when properly and scientifically analyzed, confirm that electric power was certainly available in ancient Egypt. A subsequent book of the present research project will display, explain, and analyze this most unexpected availability of electric power generated in ancient Egypt. All the details involved are not being offered in the present book as they would be too elaborate and lengthy and are best submitted in a separate book. For the moment, let it be stated that the appurtenances which were used in ancient Egypt were conducive for a careless bystander to be electrocuted and irradiated, all at the same time.

There is an additional small detail which the vast majority of the ancient Egyptians did not understand: the "false beard". In most of their murals, they depicted the Gods and the Kings as wearing a "false beard." In the case of Tutankhamun, he was wearing a faulty "fake beard," without understanding why he was supposed to wear one, except that it was considered to be a sign of divine power endowed to royalty. The correct "false beard" is shown in Fig. 5. It depicts a squarish block (most probably made of wood), that was meant to completely fill in the space between the chin and the upper chest of an individual. The realistic reason for such an unusual appendage was to stop the head from being severely jolted downwards if the person was struck by a relatively mild bolt of electricity. The block would stop the head from suddenly hitting the chest—an action that would break the neck of the victim.

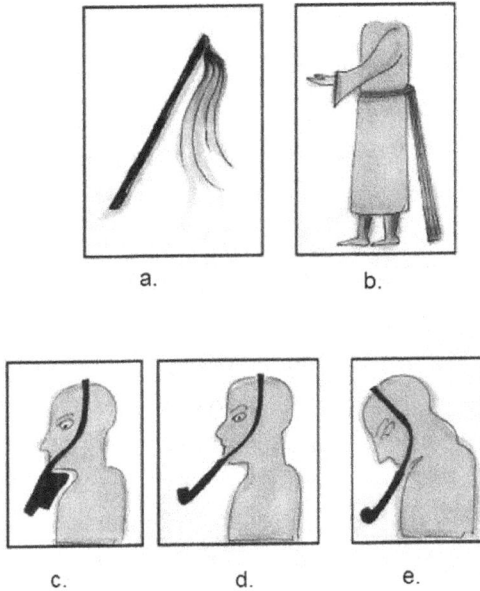

Fig. 5 - Safety devices used in ancient Egypt. (a) Flail; (b) Tail; (c) Proper chin rest, filling up the space between chin and breast; (d, e) Faulty "beard", not protecting the head from hitting the chest.

Instead of a proper "false beard", Tutankhamun, as well as others, wore a weak, though artistically stylized type of "false beard" made out of materials such as hair, linen stuffing, etc. Such a substitute for the real item, was usually shown as curling away from the chest which, under no circumstances, would protect the wearer's head from being suddenly jolted forwards and hitting the chest. The victim would have a broken neck, depending upon how powerful the jolt had been.

Egyptian lore has it that Tutankhamun had died from a blow to his head. There is some truth in this statement, although such an occurrence could not be proven via an anatomical inspection of his head. However, the confluence of the various factors determining an electric shock and electrocution, are present. We can tentatively state that Tutankhamun had been electrocuted, besides the fact

39

that he must have been radioactive. Likewise, some of the other Kings' mummies, such as, for example Seti I's, displayed a broken neck and burnt skin—which means that they, too, must have been electrocuted and irradiated.

Fig. 6                    Fig. 7

Tutankhamun's mask

The concept that electricity (or an electrified field) was present is not so far- fetched and is being supported by the existence of certain artifacts whose purpose is tied-in with static electricity. Besides the fake beard that had to be worn, we encounter other artifacts that helped the wearer to be protected from an electric shock.

A) A number of the ancient Egyptian Kings and Gods are most of the time depicted with a flail held in their hands. In essence, this artifact was a sort of a horsewhip with many strips attached to its end. It has been acknowledged as being one of the symbols of authority of a God, and thus extended to the King, since he was considered to have been a semi-God. Many times we see him depicted with the same

40

Fig. 8    Statue of Horamheb with Amun (Museo Egizio)

flail in his hand. In practical terms, such a glorified horsewhip has no real function in the hands of a King or a God, as neither one were riding horses. In those centuries there were no horses in Egypt.

Such a tool in the hands of the deity or the King occupied their hands which could not be used for any other activity. Some could suggest that the flail was a fly-swatter, a useful tool in an environment where flies are plentiful. However, if such were the case, hordes of servants that were always on hand, could have shooed

41

away the flies and relieve the King or Gods from such a bothersome and continuous chore.

The fact that they insisted in neutralizing one hand, meant that they found it important and necessary for the God or the King to perform the "shooing" away motion. This means, that it was a condition attached directly to the person itself that could be remedied only by that individual. If we consider, however, that static electricity was present in the surroundings of the Gods or the King, such a flail would make plenty of sense and would have served a very practical and necessary purpose. In such a surroundings, it is important not to allow the electrically charged particles to build up on a person's body. If the charge became too high at some point, it could constitute a lethal danger and end up in a powerful discharge, a bolt of electricity.

A flail was a simple but effective protective device. By snapping or whipping it through the air, or against the floor, it forces the built-up charged particles to fall off to the floor, and become grounded —they get absorbed into the earth. Doing so reduces the static electric charge for a certain amount of time, until it builds up again and has to be "whipped off' again. A periodic snapping action keeps the individual safe.

Such a protection device sported by the Gods indicates that they were humans, as they, too, had to be protected from the lethal potential hazard to which Earthlings were exposed.

B) In a number of cases we see that the Kings and, many times, the Gods, do not hold a flail in their hands, an omission that, should have jeopardized their safety. Instead, we see that they replaced it with another artifact that would have performed equally well: a tail! In the past, it had never been understood why a King or, sometimes, a God, would wear such an unusual appendage. Normally, that would have been one of the last things expected to be worn by royalty. It certainly was not a dignified trapping.

42

In many societies, such a tail would have been considered an insult, as it reduced a potentate to the level of an animal. In ancient Egypt, however, it was required and prudent to wear a tail when wanting to free the hands. A tail works exactly as a flail. For all practical purposes, it can be looked upon as a flail held upside down and placed hanging in the back. With each step taken by the individual, the tail would dangle and sway, to and fro, or hit the ground – an action that would shake off the charged particles that had clung to the person. As an alternative, it could be made long enough to touch the floor, and, thus, automatically ground the particles.

This is exactly the same concept that was applied to our modern cars, especially the older models. They used to have two leather straps dangling from under the rear bumpers, touching the road. They were placed there so as to discharge any static electricity that might have built up on the car. The flail or tail on ancient Egyptian deities or Kings performed the exact same function as our "modern" straps attached to our cars.

A typical example can be found on a mural in Seti I's chapel at Karnak (Fig. 9, next pg). This depiction offers some of the salient points in understanding ancient Egyptian realities:

We see the God Atun holding the hand of the King and leading him. Both are wearing "tails". By so doing, their hands are free to be used for other activities. In the present case, each is holding an "Ankh" (whose real purpose is still unknown) in one hand, and holding hands with the other. We keep in mind that in all ancient Egyptian presentations of Gods, they are depicted as human beings. This is underlined by the fact that even Gods have to wear the "tail" so as to protect them from electrical charges building up on their human bodies. If the ancient Egyptians insisted on considering, and

43

thus depicting, their Gods as humans, it behooves us to accept that fact and interpret their doings accordingly.

## Summing it up:

When we review the physical conditions of Tutankhamun's body, we realize that they display aspects of having been hit by a powerful electric bolt (or discharge), as well as by having been exposed to radioactivity.

*Main evidence for a powerful bolt having hit his head are:*

> 1) The fact that he had been "decapitated", his head was no longer connected to his spine. A powerful hit to the back of his head could have produced such a result, especially as he wore a faulty "false beard', one that could not possibly have saved him from breaking his neck. Such a stylized "beard" would not have prevented his head of abruptly hitting his chest. As a result, the report we inherited via the vague ancient Egyptian lore is correct. The young King died because of a hit to his head which then created further problems.

> 2) The chances are that such a break had not occurred when Carter tried to extract the mummy out of its sarcophagus. We observe that other Kings' mummies were also found to display the same conditions.

> 3) An autopsy showed that Tutankhamun had a broken leg. Such a situation ties in with a powerful jolt to his head, one that would make him fall and break his leg.

Fig. 9    God and King holding hands, each wearing a "tail"

### Main evidence for exposure to radioactivity are:

1) The young King had lost his hair. This aspect is a typical, recognized symptom displayed by people that have been irradiated. It cannot be assigned to the effect of a hit by an electric shock.

2) Blackened skin: Normally, this, too, is the after-effect of exposure to powerful dosages of radiation.

3) His mummy's bandages were carbonized. They fell apart when touched. These cloth strips were wrapped around his irradiated body, after his death. This means that he had been exposed to a powerful source of radiation before dying. The bandages would have absorbed radiation and its accompanying heat waves from his dead body and, thus, become carbonized.

As we analyze all these aspects, we realize that both causes contributed to this young King's death. Unfortunately, we do not know for a fact the sequence of events that had taken place before the unexpected accident occurred. Naturally, many theoretical scenarios can be conjured by fiction writers.

CHAPTER THREE

# THE TOMB

There is a thought-provoking aspect about Tutankhamun's tomb. Fig. 10 submits the general layout of the various rooms within this underground construction. The entrance is at point "A" where a downward staircase leads into a level corridor. When Carter penetrated into this tomb, the areas were separated by a stone wall, built with smallish individual stones held together by mortar. At the end of the corridor, another similarly mortared stone wall was encountered. After punching a hole into it, Carter found himself entering into the so-called Antechamber, filled with various strewn artifacts.

Around the walls of this room, patched-up sections of the wall could be seen on the west and north sides, which indicated that additional rooms were probably located behind those two patches. In fact, after breaking through these wall-sections, Carter discovered the Annex and the Tomb-chamber.

Fig. 10 *(next page)* displays the positions of these four patched-up stone walls. One peculiar aspect stands out. These four stone walls created independent, isolated rooms, three of them hermetically sealed from its neighbors. Obviously the patched-up walls indicated that, sometime in the ancient past, these rooms had been entered into after the burial took place, and then resealed. Of course, Egyptologists concluded that "thieves" had entered the premises. The latter did not seem to care that a mortared small section of the walls would certainly indicate that another room was hidden behind, and thus guide future "thieves." Their only interest seems to have been the proper separation and isolation of the rooms. In all four

47

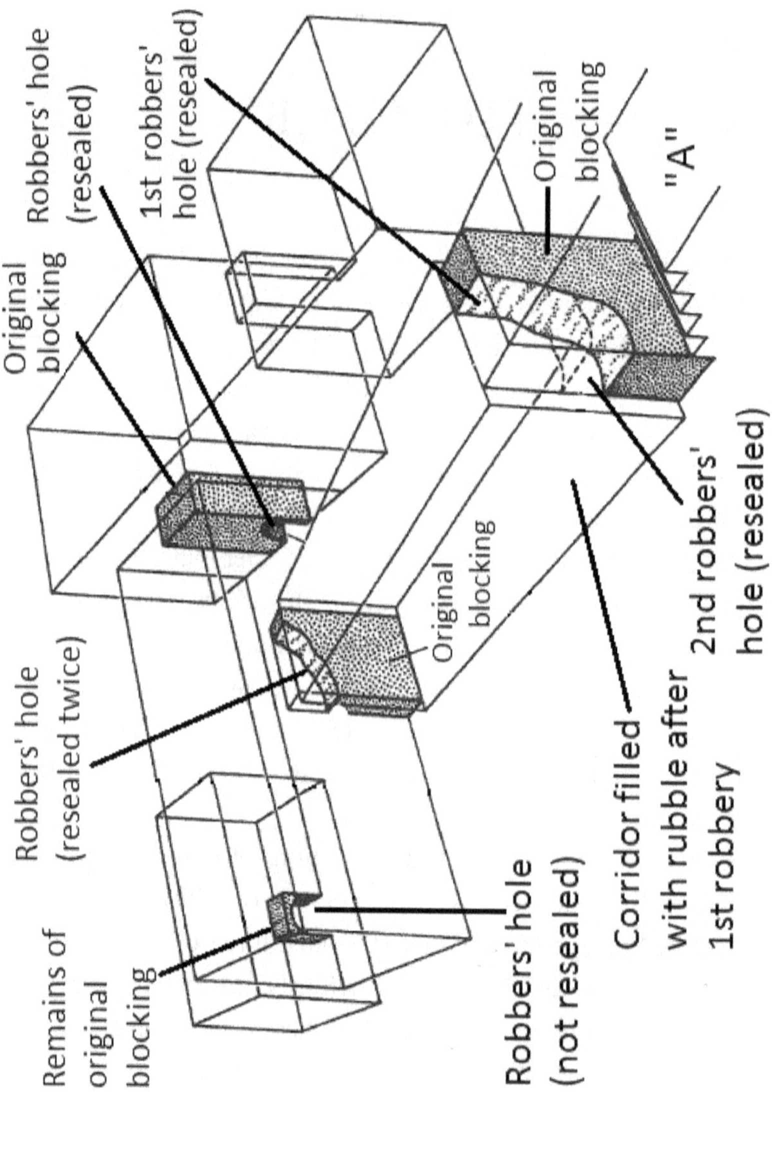

Robbers' hole (resealed)

Original blocking

1st robbers' hole (resealed)

Original blocking

"A"

Original blocking

2nd robbers' hole (resealed)

Robbers' hole (resealed twice)

Original blocking

Remains of original blocking

Robbers' hole (not resealed)

Corridor filled with rubble after 1st robbery

Fig. 10    Tutankhamun's tomb

rooms, archaeologists found total disarray and disorder, with all the items thrown around, heaped indiscriminately on top of each other and strewn around the floor. This is certainly not what one would have expected from a royal burial place. It gave the impression that somebody raged through the contents in an illogical fashion, throwing things around, as though they were only searching for something very specific and discarding what was not of their interest. Of course, the first explanation submitted by Egyptologists was to suggest the hurried activities of "thieves" who were short of time. Desroches-Noblecourt (1978) referred many times to this explanation:

*"... disordered condition was evidence of thieving" (84)*

*"...piled up ... by the grave-robbers ..." (90)*

*" .. plastered-over openings showed that the thieves had passed there ..." (68)*

*"...moved there by the thieves ... simply been dumped without any plan or pattern..." (90)*

Yet, on the other hand, she also observed:

*"...immense shrine of gilded wood ... which the archaeologists found did not seem to have been pillaged." (58)*

*"The doors ... had not been opened since the burial..." (71)*

*"Within the second shrine was a third, its seal also unbroken." (71)*

In all these four rooms, immense wealth of gold, silver, jewels, and precious artifacts were thrown around haphazardly all over the place. We also observe that the entrances to the Antechamber, Annex, and Coffin-room, show obvious signs of having been penetrated after the burial and resealed with plastered-over stones.

There is something illogical and unreal in this entire picture. Normal "thieves" penetrate into graves in order to steal valuables, objects that have a resale value. They would hardly leave a mountain of wealth and properly reseal the place before running away. In the present case, we observe that some-body did actually reenter, by punching access-holes into the inside walls, supposedly ransacked through veritable hordes of gold, jewels, and other treasures, rampaged through all the objects, left most (?) of this wealth in place, and then were thoughtful and meticulous enough to spend an inordinate amount of time to properly rebuild the torn-down inside walls, plastering them and pressing one of Tutankhamun's seals into the wet plaster. As though this was not enough and time consuming, they then resealed the outer entrance to the grave in such a masterful manner that it could not be found for 3,200 years! Such are not the typical actions of thieves salivating after treasures. It is obvious that theft, in the ordinary sense of the word, has to be discarded as a motive.

Although it is obvious that somebody did, in fact, reenter the place, it is just as obvious that gold and jewels were not their aim. We, nevertheless, must conclude that they were trying to locate "something" much more valuable to them. In their anxiety to find that special "something", they might have thrown everything around.

What was so valuable?

This peculiarity of tombs being broken into but not being plundered of their wealth is not unique to Tutankhamun's case. We observe that the same situation was repeating itself in some other tombs. For example, in 1914, Petrie and Brunton excavated around the pyramid of Lahun, supposedly belonging to King Senwosret II. They discovered a number of shaft tombs. In tomb No.8, they observed that the burial chamber was in shambles and all the contents were in complete disarray, thrown all over the place. Among that mess, a wealth of jewels and gold pieces were located, including the royal crown, amethysts, 9,500 beads, etc. Brunton, in his report (1920), indicated that this was probably the largest collection of valuables that had been found in a tomb up to that date. His report is 44 pages long of which 18 pages enumerated and described some of these jewels. And yet, there was clear evidence that this tomb had been broken into during ancient times. Another example can be cited in the excavations undertaken by George A. Reisner who in 1925-1927, discovered an untouched shaft tomb that had been dug into the desert sub-soil, south of Khufu's pyramid. The burial chamber contained a sealed alabaster sarcophagus, and a great many valuable artifacts, all thrown around helter-skelter, and mostly broken. T. G. H. James (1972, 48-49) described the scene:

> "At one side of the burial chamber stood a fine rectangular alabaster coffin on which lay gold-covered poles and beams which apparently belonged to a canopy of some kind. Other poles had fallen into the space between the coffin and the wall. The floor was covered with a mass of broken objects, parts of gold-covered furniture, copper and stone vessels, great quantities of pottery, and, everywhere, fragments of gold from unidentifiable objects. This jumble of material lay in a roughly cut chamber about fifteen feet deep, eight feet wide, and six feet high The floor was completely covered with the debris of what had been an impressive collection of funerary equipment. There was no chance of entering the chamber while it was in this state ... The whole chamber was in chaos ... The burial belonged to Queen Hetepheres, the wife of Sneferu, and the mother of Cheops."

It should also be pointed out that coffin did not contain human remains. No mummy. No coffin. No skeleton, not even remnants.

These examples again hint at the fact that something most unusual was happening in ancient times: properly sealed tombs that had remained untouched and intact for past millennia, someone had entered them, probably shortly after burial, messed up most of the items in sight, and then properly resealed the tomb so masterfully that it remained undetected during the ensuing thousands of years. Theoretically, the entire exercise of breaking into a grave was the acquisition of valuables and yet, these "robbers" did not abscond with the jewels and gold. They left them behind! Carter (1972, 42) expressed his amazement:

> "... here everything was in confusion, just as they left it. Nor did it take much imagination to picture them at their work. One—there would probably not have been room for more than one had crept into the chamber, and had then hastily but systematically ransacked its entire contents, emptying boxes, throwing things aside, piling them one upon another, and occasionally passing objects through the hole to his companions for closer examination in the outer chamber. He had done his work just about as thoroughly as an earthquake. Not a single inch of floor space remains vacant, and it will be a matter of considerable difficulty, when the time for clearing comes, to know how to begin. So far we have not made any attempt to enter the chamber, but have contented ourselves with taking stock from outside. Beautiful things it contains, too."

There is an additional aspect that is not usually stressed in the literature on this tomb, and yet it is of importance. Carter reported that each of the four plastered sections covering the four door blockings displayed a great many seal impressions whose dimensions, on average, were about 5.5 x 2.5 inches, surrounded by an oval border, in the form of a cartouche. Originally, these impressions were probably carved on wooden blocks which were then pressed onto the wet plaster. There were dozens of impressions all over the blocking sections.

Seven different types were counted by Carter. A careful examination of these mortared sections indicated that a small area had been re-plastered on each of the interconnecting walls. The re-plastered sections had also been imprinted with the oval seal cartouche. It means that whoever entered the place must have had access to at least one of the seals. Such a ready availability of the matrix tends to indicate that only a relatively short period of time could have elapsed between the original construction and the re-entry. Carter reached the same conclusion, albeit based on different evidence:

> *"From later evidence we found that this re-sealing could not have taken place later than the reign of Horemheb, i.e. from ten to fifteen years after burial." (Carter 1972, 235)*

Carter expressed surprise that these re-entries were made through very small holes, opened in the masonry, "just wide enough to admit a boy or a slightly built man" (Carter 1972, 40). He repeated this description when referring to the breach in the wall of the Antechamber, describing it as "a very small hole" (Carter 1972, 60). This surprising observation repeats itself in various other tombs. One gets the impression that in a great many cases, these builders or re-entering "thieves" were employing children, or very small people, or even baboons.

Carter considered "that there had been two successive openings and reclosings (Carter 1972, 33). Reeves (1990, 95-96), too, acknowledged that there had been a "first robbery" and a "second robbery", basing his belief on the first plastered blocking and the remortared sections of the same spots. Both archaeologists submit this conclusion in assertive terms, implying that other possibilities were ruled out. And yet, their conclusions are not necessarily correct. It could well be that the first blocking was put in place by the very same builders who excavated and set up the various chambers. In such cramped quarters, the most effective method of isolating the rooms from each other would have been to build most of the blocking wall, leave an exit hole for the very end which would then be filled in.

It is not logical to expect that the first group of "robbers" entered and ransacked the place, an action that weighed on their conscience to such an extent that they spent an inordinate amount of time in erecting the four blocking walls before leaving! A thief, whose aim is to steal, would not build internal walls that could not be seen from the outside. From a thief's point of view, what advantage is there to repair such internal stone walls? One can understand that, perhaps, they might have wanted to close up the outside entrance wall, if at all, but hardly internal separations. Thus, one could be inclined to conclude that these first blockings were created by the original builders after the burial took place and before they sealed up the place.

A relatively short while thereafter, a reentry took place. Small sections of the blockings were chiseled away in all four separating walls, giving access to all the rooms. This could be considered to have been the one and only reentry into the tomb.

However, we are confronted with a peculiar situation: intruders supposedly left the place in a mess, but decided to properly fill the breaches so as to isolate the chambers from each other. Seemingly, this must have been their aim

For clarity's sake, it should be pointed out that only three of the four breaches had been repaired (Fig. 10). The fourth one was not—the one connecting the Annex to the Antechamber. When comparing the sizes of the four openings, we observe that this one was the smallest one. In fact, one wonders how an able-bodied grown-up adult could have squeezed through such a small aperture in the masonry. We do not know why this small opening had not been repaired. In view of the fact that the entire scene displayed one of haste, it could be that the intruders did not want to spend more time in these chambers than absolutely necessary. They withdrew before finishing the repairs to the masonry wall.

Reeves (1990, 95) submitted as proof for a "first" robbery the fact that the corridor, leading from the staircase to the Antechamber had been filled with rubble and stones, from floor to ceiling. Beneath the fill, Carter observed a number of fragments of objects belonging to some of the artifacts stored in some of the chambers. This led him to conclude that the ransacking occurred first, and then the rubble was shoveled into the corridor. This is a logical conclusion and could be one of the explanations, but not necessarily the only one. It could be argued, for example, that while bringing in the artifacts through the corridor, some pieces might have broken off and dropped to the floor. The rubble was then heaped on top.

There could be many theoretical explanations for the same set of facts. Whether one or two groups of "thieves" reentered the tomb is really not germane. The important point is that, before exiting, these so-called "robbers" reconstructed the breaches in the blocking walls, and saw to it that the rooms were isolated from each other, while the corridor was completely filled with stones and rubble. The idea of completely isolating sites from one another through stones occurs in the 21$^{st}$ century, when wanting to contain radiation from escaping. Having realized that said tomb had contained radioactive substances, it becomes quite clear that the managers of this site knew exactly what they were doing and why they acted as they did. As was experienced in other tombs, the re-entry seems to have been for the purpose of retrieving the radioactive substances and not for stealing gold and jewels.

As for the mess found in all the rooms, but especially in the Annex, a closer study of the photographs could indicate that, despite all, the havoc still followed a certain order. This view seems to be shared by Carter (1977, 29), who wrote:

> *"There was a certain amount of confusion, it was true, but it was orderly confusion."*

We must also realize that, even if they wanted to, the intruders could not have placed the various items in a neat fashion. There simply was not enough room to accommodate the extensive assortment of artifacts that had to be placed in that tomb. They were forced to heap item on top of item, to place them in the restricted space available. Nevertheless, one gets the impression that the original porters were in a great hurry to get rid of their loads. Did they know the lethal surroundings they were in? Under normal circumstances, they could have stacked the items in a somewhat more orderly fashion. They either knew the type of hazardous materials stacked away in those rooms or, though ignorant of it, were under strict orders given by the knowledgeable managers, to dispose of their loads as quickly as possible and exit the premises. Even if they dutifully obeyed, it is doubtful that they escaped without damage to their health.

We probably have further evidence that the unexpected burial had proceeded in a hurry, given that the King had suddenly died at a very young age:

The second gilded shrine had been re-inscribed. Originally, it carried a name that had ended in "aten", over which the name of Tutankhamun had been incised. This could indicate that perhaps the shrine had been inscribed very early on in his reign when his name had been Tutankhaten.

The sarcophagus was carved out of a hard, yellow quartzite stone block. However, the lid "... was of red granite, painted to match the yellow of the sarcophagus box." Surprisingly, the lid was broken across its entire width. The fact that two very different qualities and colors of stones had been used, added to the observation that the lid was broken, could hint at the fact that, originally, these two pieces were not a pair. Perhaps they had started with a matched set but, due to an accident, the lid broke. It is even possible that due to the unexpected death of the King, there had been no time to fashion a new sarcophagus with its corresponding lid. Instead, they picked up whatever lid they could find in a hurry, whose dimensions fit the sarcophagus.

Nevertheless, the fact that the lid was found to be slit or broken across its entire width is of great importance.

We noted that the sarcophagus was made of yellow quartzite while the lid had been fashioned from red granite. In the vast majority of cases, sarcophagi and lids used to be made of the same type of stone. Theoretically, we could assume that when the original lid was carried into the tomb, it broke in such a way that it could no longer be used. The only replacement they could locate was made of a different type of stone. Such a solution might have been plausible were it not for the fact that the lid finally used was found by the archaeologists to be also broken across its width. Can we assume that this second lid had been in one piece when originally received? Such an expectation is logical, but not necessarily true. There could be arguments to the contrary.

Marianne Eaton-Krauss is of the opinion that the lid was already split when placed on the sarcophagus. She had written a book analyzing the sarcophagi in Tutankhamun's tomb. (1993). In an article published in KMT (2010, v21-1 P 27-28) she summarized her point of view:

> "Until it was needed, the sarcophagus lid—or rather the two pieces of it—could have lain on the floor at the south end of the Antechamber. There is a dovetail cutting for a dowel, to effect a repair on the underside of the lid, which suggests it was broken before it was brought into the tomb."

This would indicate that this lid had been split before reaching Tutankhamun's tomb, after it had been used in some other tomb. The fact that it was broken across its width suggests that it had originally been used to cover a sarcophagus that had contained radioactive substances emitting radiation as well as its accompanying waves of intensive heat.

Under normal circumstances a lid has an approximate width of about 5 ft (1.25 m) with a thickness of circa 4 in (10 cm).What magnitude of power had to have been used so as to break such a piece of granite?

Some 3300 years ago, ancient Egyptians used only wooden mallets or stone pounders along with copper chisels. Their only source of power was human rnuscle power. There is no possibility that they could have split such a piece of a granite slab all along the full 5 ft width, given the type of tools and source of power they possessed. But, nevertheless, the granite lid in question had been sliced through! Even if they could, why would they want to break a lid? This means that completely different types of tools and source of power must have been used on an involuntary basis.

The search for a proper technological answer leads us straight to the effects of radioactivity. It is well known that stone can be split by exposure to very high temperatures. In fact, granite can be made to explode and disintegrate if the temperature is high enough. Hornbostel's handbook (1978, 688) specified that "granite .... will explode and completely disintegrate if exposed to severe heat such as temperatures above 2125°F (1162.78°C)."

At somewhat lower temperatures a granite slab will crack. The exact temperature necessary to create a break depends upon the consistency of the granite stone being tested. We must keep in mind that stones do not have a uniform structure. One cannot predict and precalculate where and how the break will occur, as this will depend upon the crystalline distribution within the body of the stone and the thickness of the slab. Yet, one thing is certain. Given sufficient exposure to enough heat, a slab of granite will split.

The break across the entire width of Tutankhamun's replacement lid is not unique. We encounter the same occurrence with lids of other sarcophagi. For example:

Archaeologist Badawi (1944) discovered the sarcophagus of Amenophis hwjj of the 19th Dynasty (ca 1275 BC), —that means before the time of Tutankhamun. While the lid of said sarcophagus had been split in a somewhat straight line, the sarcophagus itself had also experienced the same fate at its mid-point section. This indicates that the source of extreme heat must have been located within the sarcophagus itself, concentrated at about the midpoint area, radiating super-heat towards the walls of the vat as well as the underside of the lid. Such a concentrated and sustained source of extreme heat located within the vat of the sarcophagus can only have been a small mass of radioactive substance. In the present case of Tutankhamun, the sarcophagus did not split, only the lid did.

Although this understanding explains how the split occurred, and thus pinpoints the area where radioactive substances must have been present, it does not explain the reason for the subsequent intrusion into this burial site. It has been clear that somebody had re-entered the premises, and before leaving had quite nicely repaired the breach they made to enter the various rooms of the tomb, obviously searching for "something" — something more valuable to them than gold and jewels — which they left in place.

A very important question has still to be answered: what were the original intruders looking for and did they find it? In his original report, Carter gave us the answer.

Thirty-four alabaster and one serpentine vessels were found in the Annex. All were empty and all had no lids or stoppers. In fact, Carter (1972, 215) added an important adjective in his description of the conditions in which they were found:

> *"With rare exception the lids and stoppers of all these vessels had been forcibly removed, thrown aside, and their contents poured out and stolen, leaving but a small amount of residue in each vessel."*

"Forcibly removed" should indicate to us that there was a determined effort exerted to get at the contents of those particular vessels which Carter considered to have contained "oils and unctuous materials." He pointed out that a residue of some viscous substances remained on the inner walls of some of these vessels.

In the same room, 36 pottery wine jars (amphora) were also located, many of which were broken. All of them were empty. In addition, 10 empty alabaster jars were found lying on the floor of the Antechamber, bringing the total to 81 containers.

Carter (1972, 216) pointed out:

> "... seldom is an important tomb found without the presence of such jars ..."

These details are important, mainly because they reiterate a situation characteristically found in most tombs: the existence of stone or clay vessels, many of which display residues of black tar-like substances or viscous oils and resins.

It should be noted that although Carter refers to pottery jars as having been used for wine which "... had dried up long ago...," he also points out that "...there was no evidence of the wine having been stolen." It is doubtful that these jars had been filled with wine. Such an expectation would be misplaced since the inside of the jars displayed a coating of some black substance or viscous, oily material. Jars containing potable wine would certainly not have black tar added to it. This would indicate that the jars had not contained wine but some other substance.

All these observations reinforce the conclusion that "thieves" were after the contents of the jars and vessels, and not after gold or jewels. Heaps of riches were untouched, except, perhaps, as a side-action while trying to locate and extract the jars from under the amassed treasures and furniture pieces. In view of the very small breaches made into the walls to allow access to the chambers, as previously suggested, this "theft" must have been perpetrated by very small individuals, such as young children or trained baboons. As baboons are more expendable than small human beings, it might be likely that baboons had been involved.

I suggest that those empty vessels contained radioactive substances that had to be pulled out at a certain point in time. The retrievers must have belonged to the same group of organizers who set up the place since they knew exactly what was buried in that tomb. The possibility also exists that the perpetrators belonged to a new group of individuals who either did not approve that lethal materials should be left in tombs or who needed that substance for further processing.

.

CHAPTER FOUR

# THEY, TOO, DIED

*"The animal was mummified and wrapped in linen
in the usual manner. It was then placed upright in a
wooden chest which was then filled, in some cases
with gypsum plaster and in others with cement. The
chests with their solidified contents were placed in
the niches which were sealed with a stone blocking."
(Emery, 1970, 7-8)*

The fact that Tutankhamun's tomb must have contained radioactive materials could suggest that this lethal substance, being available in ancient Egypt, must have been present in other sites and used for other purposes, such as for example, explosions. If such were the case, it would follow that with each explosion there would have been a serious fallout problem. Radioactivity would have spread and contaminated the immediate surrounding areas, the air, and the waters. This, in turn, would mean that people, animals, birds, fish, and flora would have perished if reached by the fallout. Even after death, these life-forms would have remained radioactive, theoretically capable of further contaminating their neighborhoods, especially if the dead animals were left to rot on the ground or were consumed by humans or other animals. Even the people involved in collecting and disposing of the carcasses strewn around the area would have been victims of prolonged exposure to radiation.

In such cases, the experience from modern times indicates that the most urgent step to be taken is to immediately bury the dead corpses or any artifact considered to have been contaminated. Does Egyptian archaeology support such an expectation and does it supply the evidence for such a revolutionary and unexpected concept?

Historians and archaeologists were always amazed to encounter huge numbers of animals of all descriptions buried in underground pits, tombs, tunnels, catacombs, and even caves. These burials included cows, birds, fish, cats, dogs, crocodiles, baboons, hippopotami, etc. Why would the ancient Egyptians inter such a variety of animals? Why would all of them be buried in the desert of Egypt?

In the absence of a better, solid explanation based on knowledge, it had been considered that all these animals were, at one time or another, consecrated to some God and supposedly venerated by the population. As a result, they commanded due respect and preservation. Unfortunately, whenever a plausible reason was not at hand, or was unknown, the tendency was to take refuge in the hazy, mystical concepts of that society, concepts which originated through the study of the ancient Egyptians' lore.

We are naturally prone to assign all these animal cemeteries to some ill-defined religious cultic tradition. Yet, for such an expectation to have been really valid, it would have been necessary for almost all cats, dogs, fish, cows, birds, etc., that lived during some 3,000 years of ancient Egyptian history, to have been buried in desert cemeteries. To the best of our understanding such is not the case; only certain numbers of certain species were found to have been interred. It is unrealistic to expect that animal veneration extended to only a restricted quantity of a given species, while the rest of them continued to be part of the food chain, enjoyed by the very same religious believers. Even if we factor in changing attitudes and religious concepts over the centuries, or at different geographical areas, such a specific attitude, while the vast additional quantities of animals were simultaneously ignored, does not support a universal theory of animal adoration. Once again, we must remember to distinguish between overt reasons subscribed to by some religious, but ignorant individuals, and the true, realistic, hidden reasons behind the actions of a knowledgeable, rational group of sophisticated people living among the ancient Egyptians.

It is true that some animals were consecrated to a specific God and thus considered to be "holy" or "sacred" to that given deity. In our modern version of understanding, these adjectives might be translated into "dangerous" or "contaminated" and to be treated with careful respect. Here are some examples of species that are known to have been consecrated to a given God:

| GOD | ANIMAL |
|---|---|
| Sobek | Crocodile |
| Ptah | Apis bull |
| Khnum | Ram (In Elephantine) |
| Amun | Ram (In Karnak) |
| Horus | Falcon (In Hierakonpolis) |
| Ra | Falcon (In Heliopolis) |
| Bastet | Cat |
| Hathor | Cow |
| Seth | Hippopotamus |
| Toth | Ibis |
| Toth | Baboon |

To clearly understand the extent of this matter, a general overview of some of these animal burials is submitted hereunder—

## GOATS AND OXEN

Loat (1905, 3-6), gave us a number of details about animal graves he discovered in the region of Gurob. One particular cemetery was divided into two parts: one was located near cultivated land and extended a short distance into the desert. It contained mainly bodies of goats and oxen. The second burial area, located further afield in the desert, was a depository of fish.

The goats and oxen were found in shallow graves, about 1.5 to 2 feet deep. Each discovered pit contained a number of animals of the same species, placed in a disorderly fashion, either next to each other, or thrown across and on top of each other in no particular order. Such a helter-skelter display certainly does not suggest a spirit of veneration and respect for animals supposedly consecrated to a God. It denotes a haste in wanting to get rid of the dead animals, including the fact that only a shallow grave had been prepared, hinting at a shortage of time to perform a proper burial.

Some of the oxen's heads still retained a portion of the cloth in which they originally had been wrapped, or, possibly, in which they had been carried to the burial place. The various pits discovered did not follow a specific construction pattern. For example, one pit measured about 22 by 19 feet and contained a confused admixture of oxen skeletons. Another pit was only 6 feet square, holding three adult and three kid goats.

Loat made a very significant observation in connection with some of the other buried animals. The species encountered are extinct in modern-day Egypt! The goats and oxen found in those pits had long horns, a characteristic that no longer exists, as Egypt had to import the Syrian variety of these two species so as to replenish and replace the original stock that had died out. In general, the new breed presently encountered in that country has short horns.

Based strictly on the shape of some pots found in only one of the graves, this archaeologist considered that this cemetery dated to the XIX—the Dynasty (ca 1,250 BC). Such a dating attempt, although widely applied in those years, can hardly be accurate, as it does not preclude the possibility of a later-date burial in which an old pot was used. Today, we naturally have much more advanced testing procedures to more accurately establish dates.

Loat also reported having found a mixture of animals in a number of graves. For example:

A group of forty skulls belonging to sheep was found near the mouth of the shaft of one of the graves; in the middle of this group, he located three dogs' skulls. Another shaft contained at a depth of only three feet, 122 skulls of goats with a sprinkle of sheep's heads, along with the skulls of two oxen and five dogs.

## FISH

The second burial specified by Loat offered a marked contrast: it was located in the middle of the desert and contained only fish. The pits, normally deeper than the ones of the goats and oxen, were more carefully dug and their contents properly aligned, placed orderly side by side, or arranged in neat layers. The great majority of the buried fish turned out to belong to the *Lates niloticus* species, also known as the Nile perch. Many of them measured about 5 to 6 feet in length, each one easily weighing about 200 pounds, when alive. The thought-provoking aspect, though, is the fact that such fish are no longer found in the Nile. They disappeared from existence, becoming extinct, just as was the

Fig. 11   Nile Perch

case with the long-horned varieties of goats and oxen.

There was another peculiarity in most of the dozens of pits uncovered. A great many of the fish were partially bound in dried grass or wrapped partly in cloth, surrounded by, or laid on top of a layer of ashes! Among other observations, Loat submitted the following information:

> "The fish was placed on a thick layer of this [fine grass ashes] and covered up with the same material... A few specimens were found wrapped in cloth... in nearly every case where fish were concerned a packing of fine grass ashes, probably "halfa", was used as a preservative." (Pg 4)

> "Pit, 6 ft x 2 ft 6 in. x 2 ft.9 in. A single fish, measuring 5 ft 6 in. in length and nearly 2 ft. in depth, had the mouth and gill openings filled with ashes..." (Pg 5)

> "19. L. niloticus...Single specimen 5 ft 6 in in length. No preservatives had been used..." (Pg 5)

> "39. Bagrus docmac Pit, 6ft x 4ft x 4ft. After removing about twelve inches of the surface sand, a layer composed chiefly of "haifa" grass, pieces of rope and sticks mixed with ashes was revealed...Below these was a layer of ashes about 2 ft in thickness containing scraps of grass, while at the bottom were three medium-sized fish lying on their backs in a thick layer of ashes, the body cavities, mouths, and gill openings were filled with the same..." (Pg 6).

To this archaeologist, the ashes found were a method of preservation – a concept difficult to support today. Instead, one could rationalize that these were not ashes purposefully carried from the outside so as to create a soft cushion for the dead fish. Sand would have achieved such a purpose, and was readily on hand in the surrounding desert. Perhaps it should be considered that the ashes were produced "internally", being the residue of the grass and cloth that had burned inside the pit, having been exposed to the searing heat produced by the radioactivity of the contaminated fish. It is well to recall at this point that ashes and charcoal have constantly been encountered by many archaeologists who dug up human tombs and burial grounds, again pointing to the existence of intense heat within the closed underground enclosures. It is also interesting to observe that "... pieces of rope and sticks..." had been found thrown into one of the graves opened by Loat. This could indicate that even the "tools" used to carry the dead animals were buried with them. Such a step would be the expected procedure, so widely applied in our present modern society, where any product exposed to any degree of radiation is promptly buried.

The fact that some fish were buried without any "preservatives," while others displayed having been originally wrapped in cloth or grass, indicates that such burials did not follow a systematical "religious" procedure, but were handled expediently, depending upon the inclination of the grave diggers, and/or the time allocated to the job.

It should be noted that not all buried animals discovered were neatly wrapped in linen. For example, Wainwright (in Petri 1912, 27) reported that, while excavating mastabas and tombs around Meydum, he found that the shaft of grave No. 45 was filled with "an enormous mass of bones of sheep and of the *Lates niloticus.*" In this particular case, the original organizers did not seem to have had the time to properly wrap the fish and sheep. Instead, they give the impression that they wanted to get rid of the "sacred" species as quickly as possible; they simply dumped them in a deep hole they found in the ground, in the middle of the desert, possibly prepared for some other purpose.

By the time Wainwright discovered them, their flesh had rotted, leaving only skeletal bones. Neither of these two life-forms live in the desert, especially not the fish which inhabit only the Nile, located a number of miles east of that shaft. Yet, the people must have been ordered to carry these large quantities all the way into the western part of the desert and dump their loads into the first available shaft. Obviously, in time of need and danger proper protection from the "sacred" animals or fish became much more important and urgent than the respect due for their undisturbed rest.

The burial of fish in the middle of the desert can have additional connotations. A fish that died of natural causes would immediately have been devoured by the crocodiles inhabiting the Nile. In fact, it is rare that fish die of natural causes, as they are part of the food chain, falling prey to higher orders of animals, fish or men. It is also farfetched to expect that religious Egyptians went fishing on the Nile, caught a number of fish, and, instead of having a tasty dinner, decided to tread a number of miles through the desert sand dunes, in order to bury their catch of the day, in special pits. If they really were following religious dogma, they would not have used "preservatives" in some instances, and none in others.

This discovery is not the only "fish cemetery" found in Egypt. In fact Loat (1905) pointed out that this species of large perches was also encountered in mummified form (If wrapping in linen can be considered to be a type of mummification). They were also found in other regions of Egypt. The main area seems to have been around the city of Esneh, in Upper Egypt, a city which the Greeks named Latopolis, obviously because of the abundance of said fish.

We suggest that there had been a radioactive contamination of the Nile's nearby waters. Such a resulting wholesale slaughter would then be declared by the priests to be a "holy" event requiring proper burial—in the desert! We should recall an interesting aspect of ancient Egyptian religious tenets: the priestly class had been forbidden to eat fish, nor were they allowed to submit them as "food offerings" to the "Gods". Such a taboo used to sound peculiar, given the fact that the Nile was and is the lifeline of the country, and its fish provide one of the main sources of sustenance products for the population. Yet, the "Gods" had decreed that their servants, the priests, should not eat fish! Obviously, the "Gods" were knowledgeable and knew exactly why fish should not be eaten (besides the fact that Nile waters are usually very dirty). At the same time, the taboo did not apply to the average individual, who continued to consume fish. Whether they died or not did not seem to worry the organizers of these activities. If large fish died out, it is a forgone conclusion that people, too, must have perished.

In the same article, Loat also pointed out the existence of various pits containing quantities of other, smaller fish thrown in a heap into their burial sites. This indicates that, at a given moment in time, a whole batch of small or large fish, swimming in that area, had met a common accidental death, irrespective of size or species. A common cause would have been the contaminated waters of the Nile in that specific area. No matter what the cause might have been, these dead fish should have been eaten up by the crocodiles that share the same waters with them. These large reptiles are not known to be fussy about the causes of death of their prey, as they constitute their next meal. If the crocodiles swam in contaminated waters or if they ate radioactive fish, it is a foregone conclusion that they, too, would have perished. In fact, they certainly died "en masse", and had to be buried in separate graveyards in the desert, of course. This will be presented in another section of this chapter.

Loat detailed the contents of 53 graves he excavated in the fish cemetery. Almost all contained one or, at times, a few large Nile perches. Nevertheless, he noted some exceptions:

In grave No. 12 were two goats, lying side by side.

In grave No. 9 he found two "Lates niloticus' and one sheep.

Grave No.14 contained a fish of another species.

In grave No. 18 he found the skeleton of a sheep resting on a bed of ashes.

Grave No. 29 housed one cat.

Grave No. 41 was a circular pit containing one dog.

In grave No. 46 there were several fish; on top of them, the ancient Egyptians had placed a sheep which Loat considered to have been a subsequent burial.

Grave No. 50 contained the head of a ram with long horns. As such, it belonged to the earlier variety of rams, presently extinct in Egypt.

The contents of the few cited graves would hint at the following:

They found it advisable to inter each Nile perch in an individual grave. Although this fish grows to some 6 feet in length and weighs up to 200 pounds, it would have been easier to dig one large pit and dump dozens of them into it. And yet, they did not do so. We could hypothesize that such large fish would have absorbed a much greater amount of radiation than the small fish. In turn, this would suggest that they would exude a much larger amount of radioactivity, thus resulting in a much greater concentration of lethal radiation.

Rather than dump the fish into a pit, we observe that they first filled the hole with "halfa" grass, placed the dead fish on it, and, in a number of cases, covered it with an additional layer of grass. Why this was necessary is not clear. Nevertheless, it is very significant to note that a good part of the grass had been transformed into ashes. It burned up. This detail greatly supports the concept that a heavy dosage of radiation had been absorbed by the perch, which, as a result, would have emitted a great amount of heat. In a covered pit, the heat would affect the grass, burning it to ashes. Naturally, conditions varied from grave to grave, depending upon the dosage absorbed by the fish and the amount of grass that had been placed in it.

In this particular site, very few dogs, cats, sheep, rams, and goats had been interred. One gets the impression that these were stray animals that happened to have been in a given spot when exposed to radiation, and had to be promptly buried.

Loat gave us an interesting detail about grave No. 3A, a pit 6.5 feet deep and 4.8 feet in diameter. All around, it had been lined with mud bricks to a height of 3.8 feet from the bottom. Each brick had been stamped with the name of Ramses II. Loat suggested that originally this construction had served as a grain-bin. This suggests that a radiation accident had probably taken place sometime during or after the reign of Ramses II, which means, at about 1250 BC or thereafter.

On the other hand, Petrie (1900, 28-30) gave us a report on his findings in some underground catacombs of sacred animals discovered in Denderah. His findings support the expectation of lethal heat having been generated within the confines of the chambers. He encountered masses of burnt animal bones that filled corridors and some of the rooms [details of this "fire" are given in Chapter 5, "Underground Fires."]

The catacomb discovered by Petrie was basically an underground corridor with entrances to chambers, all along its length. The entire space, including the corridor, had been filled with dead animals, some wrapped in linen, and some not. The rooms contained remains of various animals. Petrie located chambers of hawks, ibises, and "various smaller birds", which suggests to us that they interred any bird that happened to be flying in that particular area at the time the radioactive cloud wafted along. This catacomb also contained bones of gazelles, cats, ichneumons, and snakes. Two large chambers *"were full of dogs, some dried whole, some loose bones,"* another indication that any animal found dead had been picked up and thrown into the chambers of the catacomb. To give us an idea of the extent of the accumulated dead animals, Petrie specified that the length of the passage was about 1,900 feet, and that his team had to remove 6,000 to 7,000 tons of rubble that had filled the corridor!

## CROCODILES

Lortet and Gaillard (1909, 295) located a vast crocodile cemetery at Kom Ombo. They indicated that these dead reptiles numbered in the thousands and were found to be buried in most of the graves. Not only were adult crocodiles up to 15 feet involved, but the same deadly circumstance afflicted all stages of growth of that species from eggs with unhatched youngsters, all the way to thousands of recently-hatched ones, measuring about 12 inches. This supposedly religious veneration-rite buried all the stages in a crocodile's lifetime found in a given neighborhood. If we discount the mythical reasons so often repeated, we are led to conclude that an entire region had been exposed to and absorbed large doses of radiation which, naturally, affected them all. Those who had ordered and directed the clean-up operation were quite correct in wanting that dead reptiles, small and large, and their unhatched eggs, be collected and buried. Of course, the superstitious population complied, probably convinced that, as a religious tenet, any "sacred" animal had to be placed underground.

Fig. 12
Crocodile

The quantities involved in these burials are most impressive. Bagnani (1952, 77) mentioned the situation he encountered at Tebtynis, in the Fayoum:

*"... there still exists a vast crocodile cemetery that is one of the curiosities of this important site....There are no inscriptions or stele, no elaborate hypogeum or building such as was invariably provided for the burials of Egyptian sacred animals. A grave was simply dug in the sand—and not very deeply—and the crocodiles were buried in it, with no tombstone or visible mark of honor. The bodies were, however, elaborately mummified, with hundreds of yards of linen bandages wound round and round so as to form at times an intricate yet attractive pattern....the peculiarity of the Tebtynis burials is that they are invariably a family group. Every grave contains two large full size (six to eight feet) crocodiles, presumably Pop and Mom, and a varying number (usually about six) of babies about a couple of feet in length...In a few tombs there is a further refinement: a clutch...of crocodile eggs was buried with the family....A rough calculation of the very incomplete records of European excavators— and without calculating Egyptian clandestine digging convinced me that over a couple of thousand crocodiles had been buried here."*

Bagnani titled his article *"The Great Egyptian Crocodile Mystery."* He, too, wondered how people had collected so many crocodiles and buried them in one place.

When reference is made to large underground tunnels and chambers housing thousands of crocodiles, the impression might be conveyed that animal burials were meant only for large numbers of one species. This is not so. We are told that very small quantities of all sorts of animals were being buried there as well. While Lortet and Gaillard were reporting burial grounds containing thousands of said reptiles, De Gorostarzu (1901, 182-183) submitted information about three individual crocodiles and their hatchlings he found interred directly in the sand, in the desert, about 1 mile north of the Lahun pyramid in the Fayoum. He hit upon them at a depth of only three feet; they were wrapped in cloth, forming two separate bundles. One package contained two crocodiles about 6 to 7 feet long, while the other had only one specimen. In the larger bundle, besides the two adult reptiles, there were about 50 hatchlings, 10-12 inches long, some still tied to the yolk of the egg. In addition, a great many egg-shells had also been placed in the same bundle.

This discovery near Illahun supports the findings of Lortet and Gaillard made at Kom Ombo even though a distance of about 350 miles separates these two locations. It indicates that the same ailment befell widely separated areas of the Nile, and that the same instructions were valid at different sites: an animal declared "sacred" had to be buried.

Lortet (1905) reported a find of crocodiles he hit upon in a cave near Menfalut. His report seems to be a later version of an encounter with mummified crocodiles experienced by Fred Peake (1930, 74-75) who, in 1878, entered what might have been the same cave, although one is not certain about it. Since both Lortet and Peake are referring to a cave "near Menfalut", it could possibly mean that more than one such cave existed in the same general area, or perhaps both men had entered the same cave but through different entry points. To conserve the flavor of the report, Peake's article stated in part:

> "At the outset I was rather staggered when I saw
> that the so-called entrance was nothing more than
> a very low subterranean passage, eighteen inches
> or two feet in height... But after about fifteen feet
> of crawling through the tunnel, I reached the cave.
> With the faint light of our candles we could see that
> the place was immense, but how large we could not
> tell... It was a limestone cave, rich in stalactites and
> stalagmites, and its ramifications appeared to have

*no end. The whole place was literally floored with mummies. There were tens of thousands of them. They were packed like sardines on the ground; they were stowed away in every available crevice: they extended along all the ramifications of the cave. They were everywhere... With the help of native boys I found, after some digging, a delightful bundle of these tiny crocodiles,... all swathed as mummies, and each one something of the shape of a cigar, and about 18 ins. long." (in Ancient Egypt, v14, 1930, p74-75).*

It should be noted that Lortet specified having seen a great many human mummy-bundles intermixed with the crocodiles, while Peake's description did not clearly specify whether any human corpses were encountered. That omission would not be surprising. Lortet, as an archaeologist, was interested in pinpointing and recognizing distinctive mummy-bundles, while Peake had entered as an adventurer and as an act of bravura. His interest had been the thrill of the adventure but not the archaeological and historical value of the finds and their precise descriptions.

Lortet's report is noteworthy as it supports the expectation about the effect of contact with radioactivity. The above-mentioned cave contained a great many human corpses, intermixed with those of the crocodiles. The former may have been those of individuals who had been directly exposed to radioactive clouds that invaded a certain area along the Nile. It is also possible that these were the individuals who had been assigned the task of collecting all the dead carcasses of crocodiles and other animals, bundle them, and carry them for miles into the desert for interment in any suitable location found. The direct handling of irradiated reptiles (and other animals) would certainly have influenced their health, leading to death. It should be pointed out that the above-mentioned examples of crocodile burials are not the only ones encountered by archaeologists.

For example, Petrie came across such a cemetery at Hawara, in the Fayoum (Whittemore 1914, 249).

Crocodiles are extinct in Egypt—they all died out! This is not as surprising as it first appears. Radiation can kill any living organism.

## HIPPOPOTOMI

Crocodiles live both in water and on land, although they prefer the shallow, muddy waters along the banks of rivers. There is, at least, one other animal that shares the same preference for a habitat: the hippopotamus, a native of ancient Egypt. Based on the aspects deduced up to now, it would follow that, if reptiles died out because of exposure to radioactivity, then the hippopotami, too, must have run the same risk. Archaeological finds support such an expectation. Petrie (1930, 1) recounted that some of his associates, working at the rock tombs at Qau (thirty miles south of Asyut, in Upper Egypt), discovered a great pit full of hippopotami's bones, mixed with those of other animals and even men. At times, such bones were also found in some of the regular tombs around Qau. In another deposit, filled similarly with the bones of the same animal, the hippopotami had been wrapped in cloth, giving them the appearance of a mummified bundle.

Fig. 13  Hippopotamus

78

*"This showed that the Egyptians had collected all such
bones as being of the animal sacred to Set, and had put
some of them as relics in the tombs." (Petrie 1930, 1)*

It is very doubtful that Petrie's explanation can be sustained, since the tradition of burying hippopotami bones as good-luck charms in tombs for humans, is not constantly repeated in burials located outside the general area in question. Furthermore, if it had been a true religious rite, the ancient Egyptians would not have placed a good number of them in one grave, mixing them all in one heap. One would expect that an animal sacred to a given God, would have received a more appropriate burial, in deference to the standing of that particular deity. Instead, we should consider this mass burial to have been the result of an accidental death that befell all the hippopotami in that area, at one given moment in time. The fact that a mixture of other animals' bones, and even human ones were encountered, indicates, again, the fact that whatever living organism happened to have been present in a given spot, perished and had to be buried promptly.

As was to be expected, hippopotami are also extinct in Egypt. They, too, died out!

## BIRDS

If we further extend this concept, we arrive at the logical conclusion that birds, too, must have been afflicted. There are a variety of birds that nest and live along the banks of the Nile, or fly around in that vicinity. If radioactivity had invaded the area, it would have contaminated not only the flowing waters and the adjoining riverbanks, but also spread into the air. Winds would blow it to other regions, affecting other life-forms in near or distant regions.

As expected, Egyptian archaeology supplied us with the evidence to back up this prediction. A number of very large bird-cemeteries have been discovered in various parts of the country, such as North

Saqqara, Kom Ombo, Abydos, Thebes, Touna El Gebel, etc. These finds were made by different archaeologists, among whom could be mentioned Loat, Emery, Whittemore, and Gabra.

By far the largest percentage of birds found were ibises, with hawks following, as a distant second. The important aspect encountered was the fact that, in general, each bird was individually wrapped in linen cloth and then inserted in a clay jar. Loat (1914, 40) brought to light one of the smaller depositories. In Abydos, he came across 93 large clay jars, containing about 1,500 specimens. Although each bird had been individually wrapped, a number of them had been placed in each jar, some containing about one hundred while others held only a few. Mixed among these ibises were a few bundles of hawks, a number of shrews, a mouse-like rodent that inhabits the fields. Additionally, the remains of one ox, a few dogs, and several horned sheep were found.

Fig. 14  Ibis

The excavations at Abydos were continued the following year by Whittemore (1914, 248) who discovered an extension to this cemetery. He found 150 large jars containing more than 2,500 bundles of individual birds. In addition, a considerable number of small clay jars were also located, each holding a single wrapped body of a bird.

The largest accumulation of ibises was located by Emery, who excavated from 1964 to 1971 at the animal necropolis of North Saqqara. What he found were not simple shaft tombs or pits, but entire and huge underground catacombs, displaying all sorts of spacious corridors and adjoining rooms, "...filled to the roof with layer on layer of ibis mummies in their pottery containers...Some idea of the vast ramifications of these subterranean catacombs can be gained from the knowledge that a distance of nearly 200m. (about 660 feet), separates the entrances so far discovered." (Emery 1970, 9). It has been estimated that this repository contains about 500,000 ibises, each one individually wrapped and placed in its own clay jar (Macquitty 1976, 53).

Emery described a few details in the following terms:

> "These side galleries, on average 3 metres high by 2.5 metres wide [about 10 by 8 feet], were completely filled with thousands of sealed pottery jars...These jars however proved to contain the mummies of the falcons...Many of the side galleries were completely blocked by the many pots which were stacked in orderly rows up to the ceiling." (Emery 1971, 4-6).

We observe that, although the great majority of dead birds found belonged to the ibis family, large numbers of hawks (also known as falcons) were also present. This fact supports, once again, the expectation mentioned earlier, namely, a radiation accident would have affected all types of birds that happened to have been flying or residing in a given neighborhood. In fact, Lortet and Gaillard (1902, 20) gave us a very detailed listing of 38 different bird species which were ascertained to exist among the more than one thousand mummified specimens that archaeologist G. Maspero had forwarded to the Museum of Lyons for analysis. Out of these 1000 specimens, about half were ibises, with the remainder being a variety of birds of prey. It should be noted that Maspero had collected these samples from diverse areas, namely: Saqqara, Roda, Kom-Ombo, and Gize, an indication of how widely-spread this lethal radiation activity must have been.

As for the ibises, modern experts recognize three varieties: Sacred, Bald, and Glossy ones, all of which are extinct or very rare in present-day Egypt, even though the same name is used loosely to designate the egret.

We again are confronted with another species that used to be very common in ancient Egypt, but became extinct!

Ray (1978, 151) reported that during the ten years of digging activities in North Saqqara, Emery and his successors, Martin and Smith, discovered in that area about:

4,000,000 ibises (each placed in a container)
500,000 hawks
500 baboons

It is simply staggering to consider these quantities, especially those of the ibises, when we keep in mind that these were only the ones located by Emery in just one specific area, without taking into account other parts of Egypt, where additional animal necropolises are known to exist. Some Egyptologists hypothesized that the ancient Egyptians had a whole avian industry going, to raise ibises and hawks in captivity, kill them, mummify them (which meant, wrap them in a linen cloth), insert them in clay pots and sell them to religious people who desired to express their adoration to some God or other, by submitting offerings of pre-prepared dead birds.

It may well be that an avian industry sprang up, specifically selling "ready-packaged" ibises. Many other aspects in ancient Egyptian history, activities, structures, or artifacts seem to have had dual meanings and applications: an overt one, which the public believed to represent religious procedures and necessities as well as a covert one, manipulated by a certain class of people to suit their own requirements. The fact that thousands of ibises were found dead and had to be properly buried, could have created the idea that they were "holy" and "sacred" to the God Thoth. As such, religious respect demanded that they be placed underground in a very special manner—or so said the Priests, servants to the God Thoth.

Building on this growing belief of the ignorant and superstitious public, some enterprising individuals could have taken advantage of the naive public and established a booming business by raising ibises in captivity, killing them when a sale was made, "packaging" them "properly", and delivering them to the public to be used as a proper offering to the God. We suggest that these ibises were not radioactive but displayed the same outward appearances as the irradiated ones. The borderline between the world of reality and the one of assumed religious devotional requirements became blurred, blending into each other. The former created and nurtured the latter.

As mentioned before, in the case of the crocodiles, archaeologists discovered that even their eggs had been collected from their breeding grounds along the Nile, packaged and carried to burial sites in the desert. Such a policy did not apply to the crocodiles only. Whittemore (1914, 248) reported that during his excavations in the ibis cemetery at Abydos, among the 150 jars he opened, he found

> "A number of jars with yellow and purple bands around them contained from 40 to 200 ibis eggs, and a few hawk's eggs. Some of these ibis eggs were wrapped carefully in linen, and buried under the protection of a scarab in the form of the insect itself, Small pots were found in position near the large jars, containing mud and traces of wheat..."

It is thought-provoking to realize how thorough the organizers had been when ordering to hunt down ibis' and hawk's nests, search for and collect their eggs, package them, and transport them to the desert for burial. There was obviously a carefully planned program. They had to get to the eggs of the birds and crocodiles so as to ensure that they would not hatch and produce generations of malformed youngsters that would probably continue to irradiate and enter into the food chain. It is clear that those who were managing this entire undertaking knew exactly why they had to take such unusual measures so as to save human and animal lives.

Whittemore supplied a very important additional clue, one that fits perfectly into the overall picture of the burial of radioactive substances. Among the ibis and hawk jars, he spotted also small pots "containing mud and traces of wheat." We have claimed that the same organizers had arranged for radioactive materials to be mixed with a binding agent, such as mud, tar or resins, which they then buried in any available tomb. Egyptian archaeology is replete with examples of hundreds of thousands of jars full of dried mud, found in all sorts of burial sites. Under normal circumstances, there should not have been the slightest practical reason for jars of mud to have been buried in the same tomb as the eggs. Of course, one could argue that these mud quantities were scooped up from the river banks along with the eggs. Such an explanation could possibly have been valid, had it not been for the innumerable examples of mud-jars buried in human tombs where, theoretically, they had no business to be either. The organizers did not seem to have missed many opportunities to inter their mixtures of mud in any burial that happened to occur on a given day. Egyptian archaeology is replete with examples.

It should be noted that Whittemore obviously must have been a meticulous archaeologist who described whatever he found, even if it did not make sense to him or others of his generation. Unfortunately, many of the earlier diggers were not very observant, nor precise, given that mud is a meaningless product which theoretically possesses little if any value to archaeology. It is so common that it does not call attention to itself and, as such, is easily overlooked. Yet, mud, within the context of our new understandings, is an exceedingly important substance that can lead us to meaningful solutions of past unsolved problems found in Egyptian archaeology.

About 200 years ago, Pockocke traveled through Egypt and reported extensively on his experiences, including bird cemeteries he encountered.

> "...These catacombs are much more magnificent than the others, being the sepulchers of those birds and other animals they worshipped; for when they happened to find them dead, they embalmed them, and wrapped them up with the same care as they did human bodies, and deposited them in earthen vases covered over and stopped close with mortar.." (Pockocke 1814, 209)

This traveler's Egyptian sources seem to have told him: "when they happened to find them dead" thus suggesting that dead birds were being picked up in the fields. It is not logical to expect that death occurred through natural causes, given the enormous number of embalmed birds discovered, even taking into account a long span of time. A mass extinction through radiation absorption would make more sense. But, of course, the Egyptians of that time could not have known the real cause for such a calamity. They only knew that dead birds found lying around had to be buried in a very special way.

The fact that an "ibis packaging" industry must have been established and flourished for a number of years is illustrated by the report published by E. Peet and W.L.S. Loat (1913, 40-47). These two archaeologists had excavated at Abydos where they came across 93 large-sized jars containing quantities of packaged ibises along with few of other species.

Being located in proximity to a bird cemetery that could be dated to the Roman period (30 BC - 379 AD) and comparing the pottery found in both places, they believed that the ibis burials in question were dated to that period. While comparing pottery has been used by many archaeologists as a dating method, a better foolproof approach would be C-14 testing. It is hoped that other researchers follow through on this matter as the results could have important connotations, as will be explained in the following pages.

When we study the findings in the Abydos ibis cemetery, we come across aspects that differ from other usual ibis burial installations. The Abydos ibis cemetery was composed of 93 large, unbaked clay jars, more or less cylindrical in shape. They had been found two feet under the sand surface of the desert. It is not quite certain whether they had originally been placed on the surface of the desert and with the passing millennia the wind blew sand over them, or whether they were in fact buried two feet under the surface. Peet and Loat gave us a detailed breakdown of what they found in those 93 jars:

>About 1,350 ibises, individually packaged
>
>138 packages of feathers and bird bones
>
>100 + ibis eggs
>
>40 packages containing shrews (ca some 250)
>
>6 dogs
>
>21 hawks
>
>10 sheep
>
>6 falcons
>
>1 snake
>
>1 ox

There are some very distinct differences between the ibis galleries at N. Saqqara and the one described above. These differences can indicate to us their historical backgrounds.

1) At N. Saqqara, large underground corridors and passages had been excavated within the live rock, a very labor intensive undertaking which was necessary in order to accommodate 4,000,000 ibises. The need to dig such elaborate subterranean amenities suggests that vast flocks of birds had died almost at the same time, having been exposed to radioactivity. It is well-known that stones and rocks are the best media to absorb radiation. Obviously those who arranged to dig those underground installations were aware of the harm radiation caused. At Abydos, no such construction effort was expended. Instead a number of jars were placed on or slightly under the sand surface to store the small quantities involved. The jars contained some 1,350 ibises along with a few negligible numbers of other species.

2) In the Saqqara case, the ibises were simply wrapped in linen cloth and inserted individually in small clay tubes. At Abydos, however, each bird had been elaborately wrapped, creating geometrical designs (except for 105 units that were plainly wrapped). Each package was artfully wrapped, an activity that would have required a considerable amount of time. Obviously this was probably a paid-for, expensive service that had been extended to well-heeled, religious people who considered it important to submit an offering to their God Thoth. It is doubtful that these birds had died due to exposure to radiation. Instead, the data on hand hints at the fact that these ibises had been raised commercially to be sold to the public. For the right price, the providers of nicely packaged ibises could spend time and effort to produce all sorts of intricate designs. At least, this is one possible explanation.

3) Yet, this find could be of great interest from another point of view. Peet and Loat considered that the birds had been packaged during the Roman era. It would be important to test them for radioactivity. If they prove to be positive, it might

mean that these knowledgeable people were still in Egypt during said period of time. Such a result would throw a very important light on our past history and explain other aspects that remained mysterious. If the discovered packages were not radioactive, it might mean that these birds had been raised by a commercial undertaking, to be killed and nicely packaged for sale to superstitious people. But then, we are still faced with the problem of explaining the presence of some 100 eggs and 250 shrews. The fact that ibis eggs were also found hint at the fact that originally this finding had been exposed to radioactivity, otherwise, there would have been no reason to collect them and bury them. On the contrary, the commercial enterprise could have arranged to hatch these eggs and obtain a new generation of ibises ready to be raised and sold out at a profit.

4) As for the shrews, they were not known to have been consecrated to some given God. Why had they been packaged as though they were "Holy"— i.e. dangerous? A proper test would clarify the problem and throw very important light on the extent of the presence of radioactivity on Earth.

## LAND ANIMALS

If radiation was the culprit for the wholesale death of aquatic and avian species, it would certainly follow that land animals also had been exposed. In addition to the few examples of cat burials mentioned before, a great many other cemeteries of land animals were discovered. For example, Petrie (1901B, 46-48) reported on the burial grounds of Abadiyeh and Hu, which he excavated during the 1898-99 season.

> *"In one case a grave, and in ten cases separate pits,*
> *containing animal skulls were found... The largest*
> *deposit,... containing 138 goat heads, 5 of oxen, 5*
> *of calves, and 1 sheep's head; these were all stacked*

*in rows... In 61 was a row of goat's heads... In 62 a*
*similar row... In 72 a similar row of goat heads".*
*(p. 46)*

Petrie continued to enumerate the exact composition of each grave. Only oxen, goats, and sheep were found, in varying numbers. As a rule, one or two ox-heads were intermixed with about 3 to 8 goats and 2 to 4 sheep. It gives the impression that each grave represented the belongings of a poor peasant's small barnyard. (Perhaps, thousands of years ago, such quantities of live-stock might have classified its owner as a rich person!)

In the same area, Petrie found a dog cemetery. Some of his remarks are interesting:

> *"The dog's graves found here are also un-Egyptian;*
> *two instances were found of circular graves filled*
> *solely with dog's bodies; in another, an existing VI*
> *th—XII-th Dynasty full-length bricked grave, about*
> *6 feet deep, had been emptied, and a layer of dog's*
> *skulls and bones were put in the bottom foot depth.*
> *This is like the grave with about twenty dog's bodies*
> *found in cemetery Tat Naqada." (Petrie 1918, 48)*

Why would Petrie, an experienced hand in Egyptian burials, classify this grave as being "un-Egyptian"? Obviously he must have realized uncommon characteristics. Unfortunately, he did not specify what seemed atypical.

Debono (1951, 73-74) also discovered a large cemetery for dogs, located near Keft (Kopkos), which had been completely ransacked, displaying only some left-over fragments of mummified dogs. He located among them the skull of one cat and a number of human bones. It is surprising that such a burial should be ransacked as the proverbial "thieves" knew that no treasures and gold would have been found in it. It has been suggested that, perhaps, more recent generations dug up these skeletons in order to grind the bones and use them as fertilizer.

It has usually been suggested that the jars interred along with corpses were meant to contain foodstuffs as available supplies for the deceased for his (or his KA's ?) journey to Heaven. The evidence appears to demonstrate that a minute number of jars did, in fact, contain some form of foods, such as grains, while the vast majority did not. However, other findings suggest that the above conclusion is false. Debono (1950, 233-237) had been digging in the region of Heliopolis. He came across a number of burials which he dated to sometime between the predynastic and pharaonic eras. The human burials contained single corpses that had been covered with animal pelts or mats. No meaningful objects had been included in these burials. In addition, Debono located some graves containing single skeletons of dogs. He also uncovered a few burials of herbivores (possibly gazelles?) which contained quantities of jars.

The fact that animal burials contained jars while human tombs did not, is thought-provoking and meaningful. If we were to believe the lore that jars, filled with foodstuffs, were included in human burials, are we to conclude that animals also needed sustenance on their trips to Heaven or wherever animals went after death? Debono's discoveries offer us another confirmation that burial of jars (filled mostly with "mud"), was taking place even before the pharaonic era, a fact confirmed by Petrie.

Archaeologist Salima Ikram reported (in KMT 2007 v18/1, p7) on the dog-burials discovered by S. Harvey at the Tetisheri complex, near Abydos. She had the opportunity to investigate these findings and noted "...that not just dogs but foxes and possibly jackals..." had been interred in that pit. Once again, we are faced with the fact that whatever animals had been found dead in a given spot were thrown together into the same burial pit, no matter whether they were "consecrated" to a given "God" or not. Of course, the covert policy had not been to bury only a specific species, but to inter any animal found dead in a given locale, just as was the case in many other burials. Such repeated examples support our claim that these deaths resulted from radioactive clouds that hit given areas. Carbon 14 tests on these bones would give us the approximate year when the radioactive explosion(s) had been detonated.

Salima Ikram, who is an archaeologist in her own right, also reports on the activities of other archaeologists, via a column published in the KMT rnagazine. In *vol.19/3* (Fall 2008 p 11-12) she submitted a very interesting overview of the recent discoveries made by R. Friedman at Hierakonpolis, a site that include cemeteries of the Predynastic and Early Dynastic periods.

Ikram stated:

> "In the course of tracing the walls... the team discovered several animal burials, starting with the remains of a young baboon, aged about three years. Further along nine dogs were discovered in a pit; all save one were young and at least two were males.... Not far from these lay six cats, arranged in a circle, about 50 cm in diameter. Four of these were kittens, and the others adults. Such distributions of animal burials have been noted in other tombs. Tomb 12 contained seven baboons, a cat and a young hippo; while tomb 28 contained an adult dog and a sheep."

We are faced here with a repeat of previous burials of animals, giving the impression that whatever animals happened to have been in a given area, must have absorbed radioactivity. Noteworthy are the eight puppies and four kittens — youngsters who normally had a long many more years to live before dying an ordinary death. This certainly hints at the fact that these were not regular deaths. Whoever was supervising the general area, gave the proper instructions: contaminated dead animals (or people) had to be buried immediately. The public followed orders and performed accordingly. It is most probable that human beings were also victims during this episode and must have been interred promptly. We will not know how many corpses had been exposed to radiation unless we properly test them.

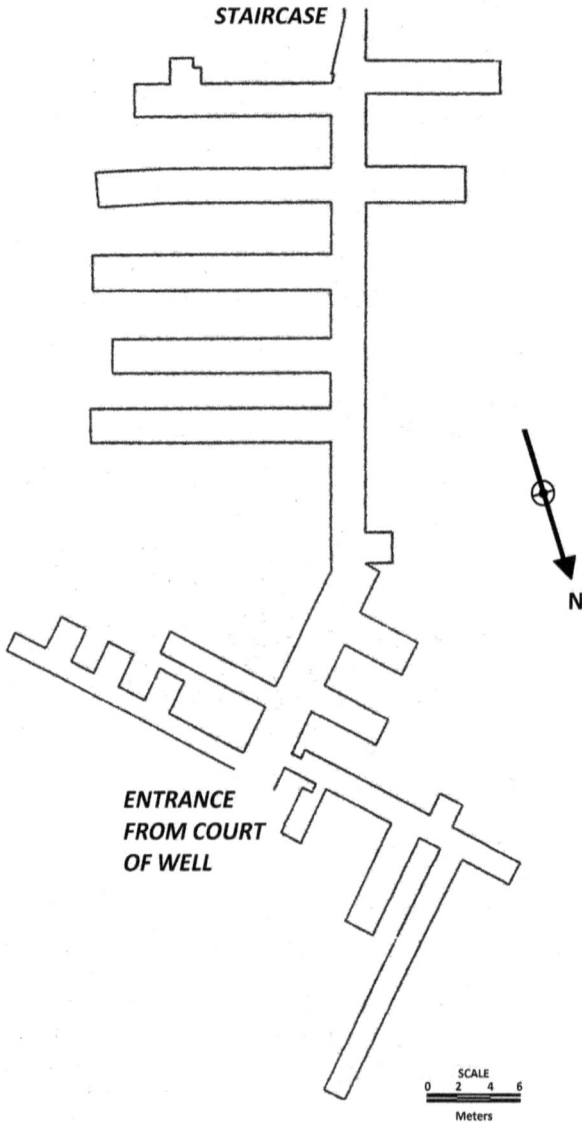

Fig. 15    Catacomb of Dogs at Abydos

Eric Peet (1914, 99-102), while digging at the cemeteries of Abydos, discovered underground catacombs for dogs as displayed in Fig. 15, which depicts a center corridor with elongated rooms extending from both sides of same. He considered that this structure had been built at two different times based on the sudden change of direction that occurs about 45 ft from the northern entrance. The chambers were described as having been "...cut fairly accurately in the solid rock, and were all between two and three metres in height" (6.6-10ft). Based on the scale shown on the plan, the depth of these rooms varied considerably between some 2m to 28m (6.6 to 92ft). The length of the central corridor extended for about 50 m (165ft). These dimensions indicate a sizeable construction that must have been prepared for the specific purpose of storing large numbers of dead animals.

Peet reported that:

> "...all chambers, and the greater part of the central corridor, were filled to within 150 cm (5 ft) of the roof with masses of poorly mummified dogs, among which were a few birds. In some chambers this mass consists of layers of dogs apparently from eight to ten deep, so that in the whole hypogeum there must be some tens of thousands." (p. 101)

Once again, we notice the presence of other species which must have been picked up along with the dead dogs lying on the ground. These few descriptions engender a number of thought-provoking observations and concepts, among others:

a- If the construction had been planned ahead of time for the expected arrival of dead dogs, they seemingly had not expected such huge numbers, to the extent that they were forced to use the greater parts of the corridors as additional warehousing spaces.

b- It is obvious that such huge numbers of dead dogs could not have been the result of their dying, one at a time. Peet (1914, 101) also pointed out "....naturally the thousands of dogs found here would not accumulate in a year or even a decade..." As shown in the previously-mentioned cases of dead animals, such quantities suggest a sudden accidental death that overcame large groupings of dogs found in an extended region.

c- This point of view is supported by the fact that the construction of this catacomb was not a piecemeal affair. They did not seem to have dug new rooms as the arrival of new shipments of dead dogs overwhelmed the established facilities. Instead, we seem to observe an original planning and construction of vast underground catacombs. Peet suggested that, at most there might have been two construction programs if we want to consider the change in direction of the corridor as indicative of such an expansion of the tomb. Even then, we cannot be certain since any addition could have been performed as a straight line extension to the previous layout. There could be other reasons, such as, for example, a change in the type and quality of rock. While all these considerations are interesting as theoretical possibilities, they do not change the basic aspects we are confronted with, namely, tens of thousands of dogs being buried at the same underground catacomb, seemingly all almost at the same time.

d- Indirectly, this situation (and other similar ones) hints at a much faster pace of digging that took place in ancient Egypt than the rate Egyptologists had considered before via the application of copper chisels and wooden mallets. With those tools, it would have taken years to excavate and create those underground catacombs. Even if bronze or iron chisels had been used, the progress would have been exceedingly slow. We must keep in mind that only two or three "chiselers" could have worked at a time due to the restricted space in which they could function. As a result, we should conclude that a much faster and more efficient mechanical digging method must have been used. Even if we admit, for a moment, that it took one year to excavate this catacomb, we are faced with an obvious problem. Until the burial installation is ready for "occupancy," what does one do with tens of thousands of dead dogs lying on the ground, waiting for their final resting place to be ready? It would have created a terrible health hazard and the fact that other animals and people would have been contaminated. The whole idea was to bury the irradiated animals (and anything else contaminated) as fast as possible before additional damage was done. This suggests that the construction of underground catacombs must have proceeded at a very much faster pace and that doing so cannot be achieved via hand-held chisels and mallets.

As for the condition of the dead animals, Peet (1914, 101) gave us some details:

> *"There is little or no bitumen used in the preparation of the mummies, and they are merely loosely wrapped in plain white cloth. The result is that those which are still intact as they lie fall to pieces at the slightest touch...It is evident that most of the chambers had never been disturbed from the day when the last dog had been laid in them, but there has certainly been disturbance at the south entrance, where lay the confused heap of bones and cloth shown in Pl XV II, fig 6"*

Concerning the date of this burial ground, Peet applied a method that cannot provide a valid answer. He pointed out having found eight Roman lamps which he sent to the British Museum for identification. Four of them have been dated to around 100 BC, while two belonged to about 400 AD, thus, a time span of about 500 years. Such a dating method can be hardly accurate as it does not tie in to the death periods of the dogs, but only to when some visitors came to inspect the place. Such an event could have taken place, for all we know, some 1000 or even 2000 years after the establishment of the catacombs along with its dead contents. As stated earlier, the only satisfactory method would be a C-14 test.

The descriptions submitted by Peet for the Abydos dog catacomb remind us very much of what Petrie (1900, 28-30) had found in the catacomb of Denderah, one that not only contained a quantity of dogs, but many other species such as birds, gazelles, cats, snakes, etc, as per floor plan he submitted. There is a great similarity between the latter and the floor-plan submitted by Peet. In both cases we observe a layout of corridors which, at one point, displayed a deflection in direction. And, here again, we consistently observe perfectly straight walls, an aspect that denotes a surprising capacity to excavate in a straight line through underground rock formations, along with, seemingly, perfectly sharp corners at the end of rooms. Such a prowess must hint at the use of tools other than simple chisels and hammers, manipulated through muscle power.

Petrie considered that the Denderah catacomb had been expanded by adding new rooms when it was necessary to do so. He determined that some of the sections belonged to the 18th, 23'd, 26th (?) Ptolemaic and Roman periods. Such a gamut of installations would indicate a great span of time, namely:

| | | |
|---|---|---|
| 18th Dyn | ca 1540 – 1295 | BC |
| 23rd Dyn | ca 818 – 715 | BC |
| 26th Dyn | ca 715 – 535 | BC |
| Ptolemaic | ca 305 – 30 | BC |
| Roman | ca 30 BC – ca 500 | AD |

This suggests an extended time period of some 1500-plus years.

Petrie, too, tried to date the various sections based on some of the artifacts he found. Here again, it must be pointed out that such a dating method, although widely applied, cannot be accurate. If one agrees that such a timing system might be acceptable as a rough estimate, it appears that serious waves of destructions occurred at various time periods, creating the lethal conditions for so many tens of thousands of animals (of different species) to have perished en masse. And, once again, this should be a very strong incentive to run a number of C-14 tests.

In 1897, archaeologist De Morgan published a map of the northern section of Saqqara in which he included the location of a large catacomb located slightly north of Teti's pyramid. His superficial investigation convinced him that those underground corridors were full of dog "mummies". No further action was undertaken since then, until, recently, Dr. Paul Nicholson of Cardiff University (England) became interested in pursuing this matter and started excavating there since a few years.

The early reports are proving that these catacombs are housing some 8,000,000 dogs and jackals—a figure which, at first sight, seems to be amazingly large. The next few years will certainly supply us with exciting details.

One of the reports issued by Cardiff University stated:

> *"The excavation team's latest estimate is that some 8,000,000 animals—most of them dogs or jackals— were buried there. Work on the animal bones suggests that they were only hours or days old when they were killed and mummified. It is likely the dogs were bred in their thousands in special puppy farms around the ancient Egyptian capital of Memphis."*

97

Dr. Nicholson, on the other hand, submitted some initial thoughts on the subject:

> *"Our findings indicate a rather different view of the relationship between people and the animals they worshipped than that normally associated with the ancient Egyptians, since many animals were killed and mummified when only a matter of hours or days old. These animals were not strictly "sacrificial". Rather, the dedication of an animal mummy was regarded as a pious act, with the animal acting as intermediary between the donor and the gods."*

This type of evaluation has been the usual approach submitted by archaeologists who had no other plausible explanation for the situation discovered now. However, the fact that very young specimens were also involved and "mummified", should alert us that we are facing the exact same situation observed in the case of the very young cats, as well as very small crocodiles, only a few inches long, along with quantities of their eggs. The present research has uncovered a much more realistic reason for all these peculiar deaths and burials: a radioactive cloud kills any animal, young or old.

It will be most interesting to await the progress reports of Dr. Nicholson, as his excavation proceeds.

Nevertheless, it is illogical to believe that the people living around Saqqara ran around all year long to catch 8,000,000 dogs and kill them, for the love of some of their "Gods." Supposedly, the same thing happened all over the vast expanse of Egypt. Unfortunately, Egyptologists allowed themselves to be persuaded that all these animals were "holy." Besides the fact that the enormous numbers involved would have made it impossible for the population to handle such a hunt—they would not have had the time to do anything else. It is not believable that they had the physical capacity to catch and kill wild animals and birds. Archaeologist

Ikram (2005) reprinted a list of these "holy" dead animals buried in Tuna Al-Gebel, including:

Wild Boars, Buzzards, Eagles, Vultures, Falcons, Cobras, Crocodiles, etc.

LIST OF ANIMALS FOUND TO BE BURIED IN THE CATACOMB OF

TUNA AL-GEBEL

**WILD BIRDS**

White Pelican
Great Crested Grebe
Shag
Darter
Common Cormorant
Grey Heron
Little Egret
Cattle Egret
Night Heron
Spoonbill
Glossy Ibis
Sacred Ibis
While Stork
African Open-bill Stork
Northern Shoveler
White-tailed Eagle
Black Kite
Black-winged Kite
European Snake Eagle
Sparrowhawk
Levant Sparrowhawk
Gabar Goshawk
Goshawk
Buzzard
Rough-legged Buzzard
Long-legged Buzzard
Imperial Eagle
Lesser-spotted Eagle
Lapped-faced Vulture
Griffon Vulture
Egyptian Vulture
Marsh Harrier
Pallid Harrier
Montagu's Harrier
Saker Falcon
Lanner Falcon
Peregrine Falcon
Hobby
Lesser Kestrel

Kestrel
Coot
Common Moorhen
Common Crane
Spur-winged Plover
Sandgrouse
Barn Owl
Eagle Owl
Short-cared Owl
Little Owl
Night jar
Egyptian Night jar
European Roller
Hoopoe
Crested Lark
White Wagtail
Carrion Crow

**WILD MAMMALS**

Greater Musk Shrew
Hamadryas Baboon
Olive Baboon
Green Monkey, Griver
Red Guenon
Barbary Ape
Egyptian Mongoose
Wild Boar
Dorcas Gazelle
African Grass Rat

**DOMESTIC MAMMALS**

Dog
Cat
Pig
Sheep
Goat
Cattle

**REPTILES**

Nile Crocodile
Egyptian Cobra
Snakes
Lizard

**FISH**

Mullet
Mormyrid spec.
Catfish
Bagrus spec.
Gray Catfish
Nile Perch
Barb
Nile Puffer

(Compiled by Dr. Ikram)

How does one catch an Eagle or a Vulture? We are asked to believe that the Egyptians, for the love of their "Gods", were able to do so—millions upon millions of times. The fact that these "holy" creatures were found in such huge numbers indicates that they had all died, more or less, at the same time and were found dead on the ground.

To convey an idea of the great diversity and quantities of animals that seemingly were declared "sacred" and placed underground, Kessler (1989, 18-29) published a twelve-page list, submitting a very detailed enumeration of the localities involved, as well as the species and quantities found buried.

This list underlines some important aspects:

1- Almost any and every type of animal or bird inhabiting Egypt was found to have been buried. It is a reaffirmation that radiation affects any living organism, irrespective of species, size or age.

2 - Each section of the country was exposed to different dosages and, undoubtedly, at different times during the past millennia. This explains the murky picture historians have inherited. Some regions considered a given animal as "sacred," while others did not. Or else, a specific species was respected at a certain point in time within a region, a condition that seemed to fade away at other times, within the same region. The areas involved extended all the way from the North to the South to Elephantine. This could suggest that all the areas where "temples", pyramids, and tombs had been active, seem to have been exposed to radiation.

3- Although a great variety of species are mentioned in Kessler's list, in many instances their numbers are very small. For example, in Hermopolis (No. 42 on the list) he mentions 4 dogs and 3 cats. If dogs and cats had been considered "sacred" in Hermopolis, what happened to the rest of their species in said town? Certainly this entire region must have had more than 4 dogs and 3 cats.

4 - In addition, Kessler also points out that eggs were likewise located in quantities, as he uses the expression:

Ibis' eggs—"found often"
Hawk's eggs—"found often"

It is naturally possible that Kessler's list is not complete, or that many another animal cemetery remains undiscovered.

In his listing of dead animals which he located in 120 different sites, Kessler specified the numbers of animals encountered. He divided them into 29 groups and named 113 different species which included 65 varieties of birds and 11 of fish. The fact that Emery discovered 5,000,000 dead birds in one location, and that Kessler specified having encountered 65 different species of birds in various sites, raises an important question: the present research had concluded that radioactivity existed in Egypt. Given an appropriate dosage, any living species would die if they came into contact with said lethal substance. There would be many theoretical scenarios that could be reconstructed to explain the death of land animals. However, when we are confronted with so many millions of dead birds, it becomes difficult, if not impossible to picture that all of them were moving around the ground when they came in contact with radioactivity. Logic would suggest that the encounter between flocks of birds and radioactivity must have taken place in the air, but hardly not on the ground. This expectation is supported by the fact that radioactivity generated on the ground does not necessarily stay on the ground. It can easily rise into the air in the form of a cloud wafting away depending upon the direction of the blowing winds. Thus, a radioactive release occurring at location "A" can produce lethal clouds that can affect flocks of birds flying some 50 miles away, at location "B". Given the massive number of birds that have been affected, such a scenario is most likely to have occurred.

While Kessler enumerated a number of serpents, we have to add those discovered by Fakhry (1959, 31) who excavated around the Pyramid of Djedkare - Isesi (V-th Dynasty- ca 2,372 BC). He found them in the ruins of the temple of the Queen's pyramid of this Pharaoh, located in the desert of Saqqara. He described his findings as follows:

> *"A part of the temple site was used for burying sand vipers; they were wrapped in cloth or put inside clay, and some of them were stored in jars of pottery. The temple of this queen is larger than any known queen's temple..."*

The fact that Fakhry found the vipers interred in the grounds of a destroyed and leveled temple of the V-th Dynasty, does not necessarily mean that they had died during that era. They could have been buried 1,000 or so years later, for all we know. C-14 tests would clarify this matter. The important thing, however, is to observe that even unimportant species, such as dead sand vipers, whose habitat is the desert, had been collected, wrapped, and then buried in the same area of the same desert. To the best of our knowledge, sand vipers had not been consecrated to a given God. Nevertheless, dead ones had to be properly handled in a safe manner, irrespective whether they had been acknowledged to have been consecrated to deities, or not. The organizers of these activities did not care about anything else, but to bury the irradiated animals.

Lortet supported the afore-mentioned general conclusions when he stated:

> *"...Based on all that we were able to observe, Egyptians mummified not only some species of animals that were directly consecrated to the Gods, but almost all the animals that lived around them."*
> *(Translated from French text of Lortet (1905, 387)*

This observation represents the logical conclusion to be expected when an area is contaminated by radioactivity. All life perishes. All animals become "sacred" and have to be buried, in some deserted site, far away from human habitat.

Emery (1969, 33) gave us good examples of what he had discovered during his excavations at North Saqqara:

> "...uncovered masses of cattle bones, some still wrapped in linen...Amidst the masses of cattle skeletons the excavations revealed a small mud-brick building with vaulted roofing. It contained three rooms....The main room was found to contain more cattle bones and skulls, many of which were covered with painted gesso. Layer on layer of these animal remains was removed."

We note that large quantities of cattle bones were being interred in the same fashion that had been applied to crocodiles, ibises, dogs, goats, etc. These masses of cattle bones could not have been the by-products of a local slaughterhouse; they would not have arranged to wrap the bones in linen cloth before burying them in special buildings.

There is little doubt that similar occurrences repeated themselves at various times and in various sections of the country where temples, mastabas and pyramids had been destroyed. Of course, not only adjacent areas would have been contaminated, but also more distant ones. Radioactive clouds could have carried the lethal substance to other regions. One can safely predict that more animal burial grounds will be uncovered, containing all sorts of species, animals that happened to be residing in a given area when the disaster occurred.

An interesting find was recently located at Abu Roash and reported by Grimal et al. (2006, 208-09). One should recall that Djedefre, the successor to Khufu, chose this area to build a very large pyramid for himself, a pyramid that has been pulverized out of existence. Said structure had a base of 350 x 350 ft, rising to a height of 224ft and containing some 700,000 tons of limestone and granite blocks. All that is left at present is a heap of stones and fragments, about 40ft high (at spots), with an estimated weight of ca 600 to 1,000 tons! Its destruction could not have been achieved by a group of laborers who, with hammers and stone pounders in hand, decided to chop down some 700,000 tons of limestone and granite boulders.

Grimal et al. submitted the findings of an excavation performed during 2004-05 by a team of Swiss archaeologists under the leadership of M. Vallogia (University of Geneva). At the southeast area of Mastaba F48, they discovered an interesting animal burial site containing more than 1200 animal "Mummies" along with very numerous animal bones, including in excess of 5000 skulls. Quantities of large-sized shrew-mice *(Crocidura olivieri)*, mixed in with smaller-sized ones *(Crocidura religiosa* or *Crocidura floweri)* were located. Additionally, they discovered rats, mice, and other rodents, as well as large quantities of falcons, ibises, and other types of birds. Over 150 "mummy" bundles were X-rayed, some of which displayed only individual bones, such as a mandible, or the feet of birds, in other words, bundling of body parts that might have been found laying on the ground, as had been located in other sectors of the country. At the same time, some bundles contained more than one species. Many remains of birds of prey and ichneumons (an older name for the Egyptian mongoose) were also encountered.

Grimal et al. pointed out that the ceramic shards found at that spot belonged to the 30th Dynasty's time, which means about 350 BC. Although this might tend to indicate the approximate date of death, we must keep in mind that those shards might have been dumped there many years after the communal death of all those animals. At the risk of being repetitive, let us reiterate that the only proper way to determine the year of death would be through

Carbon-14 tests. The results of such tests would be most important as it would give us an indication as to when these large massacres took place.

Archaeologists are continuing to locate additional burial grounds for birds. For example, archaeologist Salima Ikram reported (KMT, 201 0, v21-1, p4) the latest finds:

> *"At Ras el Gist, Z. Hawass and his team have located a large...tomb dating to the twenty-sixth Dynasty. A portion of this multi-chambered sepulcher was later used as an animal cemetery. One room was filled with clay pots containing bird mummies. This is a very southwestern location for an animal necropolis, most of which are concentrated in the more southern portion of the site. Only one other South Sakkara locale, the Pyramid of Pepi I, excavated by a French team under the direction of A. Labrousse, has thus far yielded bird mummies."*

The burial ground located by Hawass has been dated to the 26th Dynasty, which means, ca 700-525 BC (Saitic period). The one reported by Labrousse, however, seems to have been dated to Pepi I's time (ca 2275 BC) or some 1500 years earlier than the first one.

Again, a word of caution. Just because some dead birds were found in a 26th Dynasty tomb is not reason, by itself, to believe that they had died during the 26th Dynasty. They could have been irradiated 400 years later but the undertakers in charge found a handy, older underground tomb's chamber which they used to store the birds. The same possibility could have applied to Labrousses's discovery: those birds might have died and been buried at a much later date than the era of Pepi I.

## BABOONS

Among all the buried animals, one was in a class by itself: the baboon. In contrast to other species mentioned so far, the baboon has pronounced intelligence and is willing and able to learn, retain, and perform manual jobs taught by its trainers. It possesses dexterous fingers which allow it to handle objects. With appropriate training early in life, baboons may attach themselves to humans and become just as loyal as a dog to its master, perhaps even more so. Even today, baboons are being taught and used for the performance of chores, such as collecting coconuts from tall trees and bringing them back to their owners. Basically, they could constitute a cheap workforce, replacing human manual labor, tirelessly and willingly executing their tasks. They can perform difficult jobs in situations not easily suited to humans, provided they are first properly trained for them. In the hands of capable trainers they can be a very valuable asset. The baboons of ancient Egypt belonged mainly to the sub-species known as "Hamadryas," a small animal with grey hair. They are about 24-28 inches (60-70 cm) tall, and weigh only a maximum of 40 pounds (ca 18 kg).

In ancient Egypt, the baboon seemed to have had a special place. There are numerous wall paintings and reliefs on which they are depicted holding tools in their hands, and performing some sort of a job in the presence of various individuals, and even, at times,

Fig. 16   Baboon

in front of the King or the Gods. Unfortunately, up to now, classical Egyptology has not been able to properly decipher the baboon's activities depicted on those murals and submit a cogent explanation for them.

The fact that baboons were, themselves, also used as a "tool", was depicted on the murals of temples. We have, for example, two typical scenes shown on some of the walls of the Denderah temple. Fig. 17 shows a King kneeling in front of a "sacred naos", obviously an instrument of considerable interest. Usually a King would not crawl on his knees unless he was facing a God, or a substitute with special divine power that demanded respect.

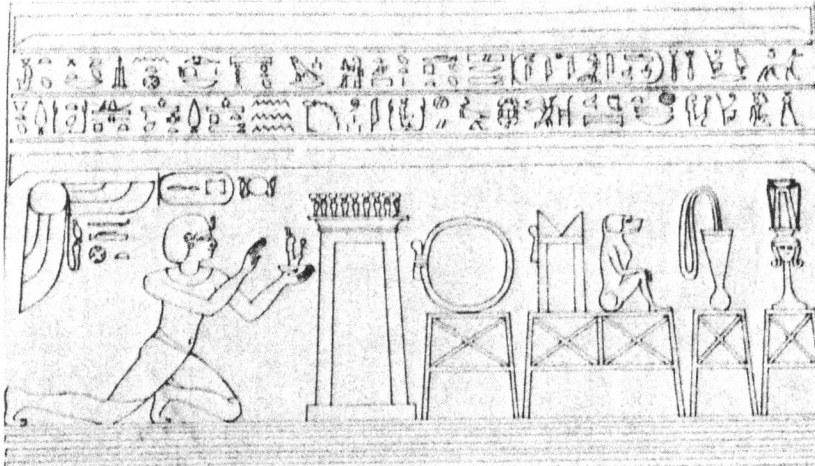

Fig. 17    A mural at the Denderah Temple, showing the baboon as a tool in conjunction with other tools

Next to the naos, we see four tables, each one displaying one of the tools being used in conjunction with the activities taking place with and around the naos. We do not know the real usage of these artifacts. However, one of the "tools" displayed was a baboon. The Egyptian artists seemed to have wanted to impart the message that the baboon was being used as a tool and/or was involved in handling some of the particular artifacts displayed, artifacts that were being used in conjunction with the "sacred" or "holy" naos. These two adjectives, as we came to understand by now, were cover-up terms for "very dangerous". The baboon was involved in some very dangerous activity. In another mural also at the Denderah temple (Fig. 18) we observe not only a repeat of the previous scene, but even an enlargement of the activities. This time they drew several tables, each one displaying a different "tool," among which we again see the baboon perched on a table. This might be an indication that the baboon was itself a tool and being handled as such.

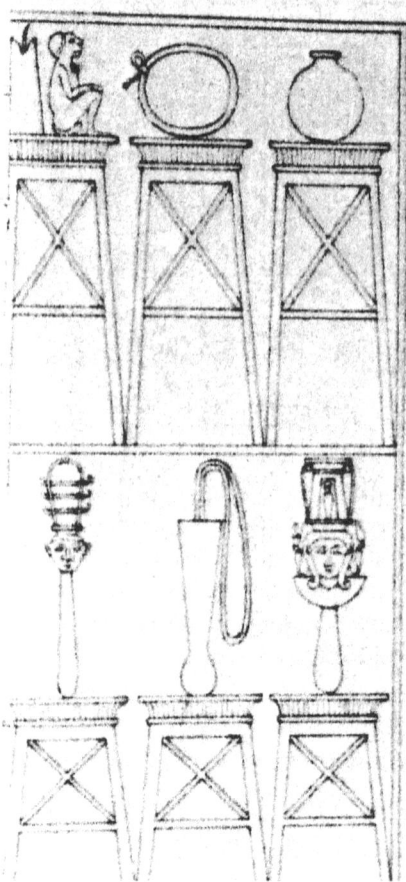

The baboons were also buried but this time very meaningful details stand out as far as the interment method used by the ancient Egyptians – a method that immediately distinguishes them from all the other buried animals. Emery (1970) uncovered large tunnels in the form of catacombs which had been excavated within the bedrock at North Saqqara. Among other details, he stated:

*"...preliminary exploration was possible, revealing a series of galleries lined with niches in which had*

Fig. 18  Another mural at the Denderah Temple, showing several tables, each with a tool. The baboon occupies the upper-left table.

*been buried hundreds of the cynocephalous baboons...These galleries were filled with debris...Like the ibis catacombs, the galleries had been cut in a soft stratum of rock, but unlike them they had been lined with fine limestone masonry which for the most part was found in perfect condition...*

*With a common vestibule entrance the galleries are on two levels connected by a stairway... In the floor in the southeast corner of the vestibule, a shaft descends to another underground complex containing more wall-niches for baboon burials, two of which were found intact, these being the only undisturbed burials in the whole mausoleum. The method of interment is of considerable interest and, as far as I am aware, unique. The animal was mummified and wrapped in linen in the usual manner. It was then placed upright in a wooden chest which was then filled, in some cases with gypsum plaster and in others with cement. The chests with their solidified contents were placed in the niches which were sealed with a stone blocking...As the debris was being cleared from both the upper and lower galleries, many objects were recovered amidst the remains of baboon mummies, the broken fragments of their burial chest and the smashed blocks of the cement which had encased them." (Emery 1970, 7-8)*

The aspects that are thought-provoking are the multiple precautions taken to properly insulate and isolate individual baboons. These burial methods were unique and, with hindsight, they were most logical and commendable, once we accept the radioactive character of the entire society.

1. First, the baboons were wrapped in linen cloth.
2. Then they were placed inside a block of cement or gypsum plaster so as to be completely enveloped by lithic material.

Fig. 19    Baboon plaster blocks, as found (courtesy Egypt Exploration Society)

3. This hardened block was subsequently pushed into a niche that had been hewn into the rocky walls of the catacomb.

4. The front of the niche was sealed by inserting stone blocks into it and plastered.

For all practical purposes, they ended up with a dead corpse, insulated on all sides from the outside world by thicknesses of stones, in which it lay embedded. At first it seems unusual and odd that ancient Egyptians went to such extraordinary lengths and trouble simply to dispose of a dead animal. Obviously there must have been a very good reason to do so.

Based on the concepts discovered up to this point, we believe that these baboons must have been highly radioactive and had to be insulated to the greatest extent possible— hence the isolation behind barriers of stone. In modern times, we learned that stones are

Fig. 20    Baboon catacomb cells after clean-up (courtesy Egypt Exploration Society)

the best protection to contain radiation. Furthermore, these animals must have absorbed much larger dosages than any of the other animals whose burial methods pale in comparison to the elaborate precautions undertaken in the case of the baboon interments.

As observed in many tombs used ostensibly for humans, here too, seemingly "thieves" are considered to have entered, ripped open each individual niche in the rock, broke the cement blocks, extracted the baboon's corpses and ran away with their trophy. It is difficult to conceive that robbers would have been interested in going to all this length just to take hold of dead baboons. As had been experienced in a great many human tombs, as well as in Tutankhamun's tomb, there were re-entries that took place but not for the purpose of stealing valuables but to extract the special lethal substance that had been stored in those underground chambers. It is most likely that those who broke into the baboons' elaborate burial set-up were after something dangerous: taking away the highly irradiated baboon corpses.

Lortet came across a different type of baboon burials which he described as follows:

> "...At the south of the Valley of the Queens, we had the luck to discover a necropolis of the representatives of the God Thot, in an extremely wild ravine situated south of the Theban rocky mountains. This picturesque valley is bordered on the right and the left by enormous sheer cliffs...At the base of these rocks, we discovered hundreds of tombs containing the remains of baboons.

> Unfortunately the pits were shallow and had been invaded by water, sometime in their past; as a result, the mummies were found to be disturbed, most of the times. All of them seem to have been prepared very carelessly. Some were simply buried within the marl that dropped from the mountains, or else

*they were placed either in wooden coffins or in clay*
*sarcophagi. Others were more carefully embalmed,*
*after being wrapped with tapes that had been*
*dipped in bitumen; they were then placed in great*
*jars, similar to those used for Peruvian mummies."*
*(Translated from French text of Lortet 1905, 385).*

Although Lortet found that the baboon corpses had been buried in shallow graves, which "had been invaded by water", such conditions are definitely not recommended for interment of "hot" bodies. However, given the site in question, we can understand why the graves turned out to be located in shallow ground. Most likely, they had been initially placed much deeper in the ground. The region in question is a desolate, rough, and very mountainous wasteland. From time to time, torrential rain storms occur, creating cascades of water streams pouring down from the higher elevations of the mountain. These rushing streams wash away boulders, stones and surface "marl," — ground under which the baboons had been buried. When the surface earth-cover gets washed away, the graves become "shallow."

As for the "careless" preparation of the mummies, the need to do so might be assigned to the urgent desire to get rid of the baboon corpses.

Author Sue Davies (2006) submitted most interesting details of the burial niches, each one containing individual baboons buried within their gypsum-plaster blocks. She gave us a great many physical details, dimensions and pictures of the extensive catacomb of the baboon burial site at North Saqqara. The following few details will give an idea of the extensive underground digging that had been performed in ancient times.

The total length of the various baboon galleries is about 200 m (660 ft). Within this stretch, Davies reported the existence of some 395 niches, each one having contained individual gypsum-plaster blocks, within which they had placed the baboons. At the same time she interpreted this data and gave us an idea of the years when these burials must have taken place (Davies 2006, 84):

| | | |
|---|---|---|
| Upper Gallery | 41 burials | c 404 - 366 BC |
| Tomb Chamber | 4 " | c 365 - 362 BC |
| Side Gallery | 25 " | c 361 - 339 BC |
| E Side Gallery | 89 " | c 338 - 257 BC |
| W Stairwell + E room | 12 " | c 256 - 246 BC |
| Lower Gallery | 224 " | c 245 - 40 BC |
| | 395 burials | |

Based on this study, we realize that these 395 irradiated baboons were performing their dangerous and lethal work during a period of about 400 years. (Just for accuracy's sake, let it be pointed out that researchers Goudsmit and Brandon-Jones (1999, 45-53), reported that there were 200 niches in the upper level and 237 on the lower level, for a total of 437 burials).

One must now ask, why would baboons have absorbed unusually higher dosages of radiation than the crocodiles, dogs, cats, oxen, etc.? Because of their intelligence, learning ability, and dexterous capacities, we claim they were trained to constantly handle radioactive objects at the direction of their handlers who needed animals with dexterity and intelligence to physically deal with the lethal materials being stored, taken out of storage, or processed. Although some of the "priests" also must have perished, the highly dangerous tasks would have been assigned to the speechless, uncomplaining animals; they were more "expendable" than humans.

Although oral traditions or written records did not tell us exactly what tasks these poor baboons were performing, archaeology seems to have given us some probable evidence which would properly fit into the overall scheme discovered by the present study.

Throughout their excavations, archaeologists usually encountered very small openings, supposedly made and used by "thieves" in order to reenter and exit tombs. Egyptologists were always puzzled to encounter openings so small they would not let a normal adult person slide through. A few examples will amplify this point.

In the case of Tutankhamun's tomb, we had noticed that a post- burial entry had taken place, as referred to in Chapter 2. Carter expressed his surprise on a number of occasions, when alluding to the very small openings he found in walls separating the various chambers:

> *"...revealed the fact that a small breach had been made near the bottom, just wide enough to admit a boy or a slightly built man..." (Carter 1972, 40)*

> *"Next...the thieves turned their attention to the Annexe, knocking a hole in its doorway just big enough to let them through... Then... they directed themselves towards the burial chamber and made a very small hole in the sealed doorway..." (Carter 1972, 60)*

Barsanti excavated at the Old Kingdom necropolis of Heliopolis. When reporting his finds at the tomb of Meru, he observed that the stone sarcophagus had been re-entered:

> *"...I was able to see that the cover was not intact: towards the southern end, they had made an opening, allowing a child to slide into the vat."* (Translated from the French text of Barsanti 1916, 214).

Upon finally lifting the cover, Barsanti found only water and mud. The latter was spread to dry and a minute examination of same revealed not a single trace of any object. (Once again mud is showing up in a tomb!). This sarcophagus had a built-in extension to house the canopic jars, "...there were found no vestiges of these vases, nor their contents." It is obvious that a strong stone vat had not been installed in that chamber just to contain mud and "nothing else." Whatever had been placed inside it had disappeared through the small opening, pulled out by somebody of very small stature. Perhaps a baboon?

About six feet further down the corridor, Barsanti discovered the sarcophagus of Sebeki, an almost duplicate situation as experienced in the case of Meru. Again, a very small hole had been made, large enough to let a small child through and, again, the contents found was only mud.

Behind these sites, Barsanti discovered two identical additional burials. When describing the first one, he stated:

> *"The thieves had employed a different procedure...in order to enter the sarcophagus: instead of making a hole in the cover, they contented themselves to lift it up by about 30 centimeters [12 inches], just enough of a space to allow a child to slide through it."* (Translated from the French text of Barsanti, 1916, 218-9)

Fig. 21    Baboon catacomb corridor after clean-up (courtesy Egypt
           Exploration Society)

Once again, not the slightest object or remnant of it was found,
except – mud! The second tomb, belonging to Kem-N-her, displayed
an exact duplication of the very same conditions describe above.

Brunton (1920) described for us his excavations at Lahun, where
disorder reigned in tomb No. 8, although a large horde of jewelry
had been left untouched in an alcove in the wall, almost exactly
the same general conditions found in Tutankhamun's tomb. Here,
however, the lid of the sarcophagus had not been lifted; instead
the intruders chiseled a hole through its end in order to reach the
contents.

Brunton submitted a photograph showing the incredibly small
opening that had been made. Such an aperture would have been
useless to a medium-sized person, or even to a small child. A
baboon could have fit through. Or else, they could have inserted a
shaft with a hook at the end and pulled out the contents.

In a meaningful passage, Brunton pointed out that when the sarcophagus was opened by him, it was empty! Only a few scraps of gold foil were located in it. If this vat had contained a wooden casket with a mummy or a skeleton, it would have been hardly possible to extract them through that small hole so that nothing was left behind. Not even fragments of a bone or wood had been found!

This situation implies that the sarcophagus had not been used to house a body, but something of a small dimension. Experience has shown that intruders knew exactly where to go so as to locate what they were after. They did not seem to have attacked closed sarcophagi in a haphazard manner—just hoping to find some treasures in it. Had it contained radioactive substances, such a direct choice would be understandable given the type of knowledge that seems to have been prevalent at that time in ancient Egypt. A Geiger counter or a similar sensor could have led the intruders directly to their goal. A baboon or its handler could have used such a simple instrument, pinpoint the location and let the animal enter through the small holes and pick up the "hot" substance. To consider such a possibility might be deemed very audacious to say the least. However, if there really were technically-advanced people in ancient Egypt handling radioactivity (and our evidence points to it), it becomes a foregone conclusion that they would certainly have had sensors or other registering devices.

Next to this sarcophagus was a recess in the wall where Brunton found a most important accumulation of gold artifacts and jewelry that had remained untouched for all these millennia, even though the chamber was found to be in complete disarray. Once again, we are faced with the same set of situations found in Tutankhamun's chambers: valuable articles stored in the open—a god-send for any professional thief, were by-passed while the "robbers" went to all the trouble of chiseling a hole in a heavy-walled stone-vat so as to get at "something" more important than gold artifacts and jewelry!

Fig. 22 The sarcophagus discovered by Brunton (1920) in Tomb 8, displaying an entry hole.

In the past, it had been considered that small scraps of gold-foil found in tombs had fallen off gilded caskets. In certain cases that might have been true, while, in other instances, there are serious reasons to doubt such an explanation. The situation at Lahun is a good example. The sarcophagus contained not the slightest trace of having housed a casket, and yet, tiny gold-foil pieces were found in it. This indicates that gold-foil must have had a function in connection with the "something special" that had been placed in that stone sarcophagus.

Firth (1928, 88) made a similar observation, while describing one of the small satellite pyramids at Saqqara:

> "The descending passage from the north side was
> found with so much of the original stopping of
> limestone blocks still in position that the small hole
> made by a plunderer had to be enlarged to permit of
> a man getting into the chamber."

The same archaeologist excavated at the small pyramid to the west of Userkaf's edifice; he submitted the following remarks:

> "The descending passage still retained a part of its
> original blocking and although a small hole had been

*cut through it, the aperture was only large enough*
*to admit of the passage of a very small boy..." (Firth*
*1929, 67).*

Winlock (1942, PI 13a) took a picture of the entrance slab sealing the tomb of Neferu at Deir-El-Bahri. It showed a slight opening in the upper right corner that would not allow a normal-sized "thief" to pass through.

Likewise, Arnold gave us various examples. During his excavations at the secondary pyramid No.3 of Senwosret I (ca 1,950 BC), he encountered the same situation, which he described as follows:

> *"The situation becomes even more confusing*
> *because the entrance to the corridor-chamber*
> *was discovered sealed with the original horizontal*
> *limestone slabs, which thieves had broken only*
> *enough to squeeze through... the first door of the*
> *tomb consisting of a huge limestone slab fitted into*
> *a limestone doorframe...a hole just large enough*
> *to admit a slim man had been opened in the upper*
> *right corner." (Arnold 1992A, 28)*

In secondary pyramid No.2 of the same King, Arnold came across a repeat of the situation depicted by Brunton. A very small hole had been chiseled through part of the sarcophagus and its cover. It is doubtful that even a small child could have entered through such an opening. A photograph submitted by Arnold (1982, PI 7d) showed the minute intrusion-hole found in the blocked entrance to the south tomb of Amenemhet III's pyramid at Dahshur (ca 1,800 BC).

These and many other similar examples support the belief that neither an adult, nor even a child old enough to know what it was doing, could have availed themselves of such insignificant entry holes. On the other hand, however, a trained baboon would have found these holes sufficiently large to enter, perform its taught and assigned manual job, and exit. Their tasks, for which they would have been trained, could well have been to retrieve and bring back radioactive substances. Their handlers knew exactly what was involved and how lethal the operation was. The fact that many tombs had been reentered, messed up, jars broken, furniture thrown around (while jewels and gold artifacts were skipped), could probably indicate that baboons had been at work—they were only taught to fetch the radioactive items and not any valuable items which they could throw around.

There is, naturally, the additional possibility that these holes were made large enough to allow mainly the insertion of a wooden or metal shaft with a hook at its end. Such a tool would have been used to pull out a small container located within the "sarcophagus," a vessel that contained the radioactive substance. The fact that no human remains were usually located within these vats, gives support to the above-mentioned concept. In fact, in a good many pictures of Gods and, sometimes, of Kings, we see them holding in their hands a long shaft with hooks at their ends. At times they were depicted holding even two different types of shafts with hooks on their ends.

Another glaring example was submitted by archaeologist Aidan Dodson (1998, fig 339) as shown in Fig. 23. He reported that said sarcophagus belonged to an individual named Weta, which he dated to the late Old Kingdom's time (probably 2300 to 2100 BC). This picture—as well as the previous quotation—are two very important points that must always be kept in mind:

a)  The height of Weta's sarcophagus is probably about 1 m (3.3 ft). Proportionally, the thickness of the cover would be about 25 cm (10 in) One could calculate the enormous power that would have been necessary to chisel an opening through such a thickness of limestone. Yet, the perpetrators of this action must have found it easier and simpler to do so, rather than twist around the cover— an action that had been performed in many another case. We are naturally entitled to ask ourselves: what happened to the corpse that originally resided in the cavity of said sarcophagus? We don't know. Perhaps no dead body had ever been placed into the sarcophagus.

b) Once again, the reader must be warned that this break-in action we see depicted did not necessarily take place towards the late Old Kingdom's time. Although the sarcophagus had been created during said period, we must not conclude that the break-in did also occur at that time. For all we know, this event might have taken place some 1000 years later.

Fig. 23    Sarcophagus of Weta (Late Old Kingdom)

The constant contact with lethal substances would naturally take its toll on those poor animals. They would have died an excruciating death. Their bodies would have been highly radioactive, which explains the most unusual precautions taken by the knowledgeable organizers when burying the baboons inside gypsum blocks, which, in turn, were then enveloped on all sides by depths of stone.

Since the baboons had been exposed to radioactivity, they were also declared "Holy" or "sacred" to the God Thoth, the same God to whom the ibises had been consecrated.

Goudsmit and Brandon-Jones (1999, 45-53) gave us information that might constitute a clue about the baboon's activities. They examined the baboon catacomb of Saqqara and offered the following observations:

1- The construction of that particular catacomb seems to have begun in about 400 BC, although earlier burials are known to have taken place in *"disused tomb chambers in the cliff face in the sixth and fifth centuries BC."*

2- This site contained 200 monkey-niches on the upper level, with an additional 237 units on a lower level, for a total of 437 burials. Most of these niches had been broken into and their contents taken out or destroyed. (Could this have been another instance of extracting a "hot" item that had been buried, as had been the case with many of the reentered tombs?)

3- Of the 143 baboons examined, it was established that 83% died at an age of less than 13 years. The breakdown depicts a more thought-provoking picture:

| | |
|---|---|
| 55% died as adults | (6.5 years old or older) |
| 20% died as subadults | (5.5 - 7.5 years old) |
| 20% died as adolescents | (2.5- 7.5 years old) |
| 4% died as juveniles | (15- 33 months old) |
| 1% died as infants | (Less than 21 months old) |

And yet, it is known that these primates have a normal life span of about 40 years! This means that their normal life expectancy had been greatly reduced.

4- The ratio of males to females was 2 to 1

5- These two researchers concluded that "...the preponderance of males and the scarcity of infants and juveniles suggest solitary confinement, with few breeding opportunities."

6- 82% of the examined baboons displayed abnormal development of their dental and skull-bones which could suggest a deficiency in calcium or vitamin D. Hollick (1996) had shown that primates obtain their vitamin D through the ultra-violet light supplied by sunshine and not through food intake.

Such a situation would make sense if we realize that the baboons spent most of their time as a "tool" of their masters, inside the windowless, dark "temples" and in underground burial chambers. Nevertheless, the fact that their lives were drastically shortened by a very significant percentage, would hint at an additional factor pinpointed by this study, namely, the type of work they were forced to perform.

Further interesting details were submitted by Kessler (1987) in connection with his examination of bones and skeletons. In some of the simians evaluated, he found deformities in their bones, especially in the extremities of leg and arm bones. In addition, the bone thickness was thinned, giving the impression that these animals must have suffered from osteoporosis. Other Egyptologists consider that the deformities could be assigned to rheumatism since these poor baboons were understood to have been spending a good part of their lives within dark, sunless, and probably humid surroundings within tombs and/or Temples.

Two other archaeologists, Lortet and Gaillard (1909) mentioned that they found skeletons of baboons which must have suffered terribly from a case of advanced arthritis since a great many of their vertebral disks, and even those in their tails, were completely fused to each other.

An overview of the various aspects encountered point to the very same evidence as observed in a number of human burials, such as Tutankhamun's tomb, or Sekhemhet's burial chamber located in his pyramid, or some of the royal tombs in the Valley of the Kings. In each case we are expected to believe that "thieves" broke into the sites, "stole something" (but not gold and jewels), utterly destroyed the premises in question, and ran away only after sealing off the main entrances and/or exits by boarding them with stone blocks! In essence they acted most responsibly by spending time and effort to seal the exits of the premises — exactly as they did in the case of the baboon's catacomb, thus isolating radioactivity within the premises and hindering it from leaking to the populated, outside world. Such an action can only be expected from very knowledge-able and sophisticated people (not "thieves") who knew exactly the lethal dangers of radioactivity. This suggests that those who built, used and then destroyed the various dangerous sites, did their best to protect future generations of the local population from entering and using those boarded and abandoned radioactive premises.

There is an additional sad but thought-provoking ending to the saga of the baboons. Today, their species is extinct in Egypt. They all died out because they could not reproduce as a healthy, surviv-able class of animals.

## SHAM MUMMIFICATION

Some archaeologists submitted information that indirectly hinted at the thoroughness of the cleaning-up operations that had taken place after each radiation episode. Ginsburg (1999, 183-191) performed a study that focused on the burials of cats in Saqqara. He reported having found various types of "mummified" packages, some representing the normal lengths of cats, while others were only about 6 inches long. Some of the latter contained only cat's body-parts, such as one feline's leg that had been cut off from the body, or only a tail. Some had portions of birds and reptiles. One package even contained two hind legs of a frog. Another package included six small kittens. Such an agglomeration of individual body-parts of cats, including those of other species, are thought-provoking. If the cats were supposed to have been consecrated, killed, and offered to the God Bastet, why were other species' parts mixed in? Were they trying to cheat the God by offering make-believe cat-mummies? Or were they trying to cheat the public by supplying them with sham packages?

In addition, Ginsburg noticed that in a number of cases where whole cats had been mummified, the animals had been killed via strangulation. He found that their heads had been twisted by about 90 degrees in relation to their spines.

The same observation had also been made earlier by Armitage and Clutton-Brock (1981, 185-196) who X-rayed 53 cat-mummies at the British Museum of London. Besides confirming that many cats had twisted heads, this British team analyzed their age distribution. They established the following breakdown:

| | |
|---|---|
| 2 | less than 1 month old |
| 20 | 1 to 4 months old |
| 5 | 5 to 8 months old |
| 17 | 9 to 12 months old |
| 7 | 13 to 24 months old |
| 2 | over 24 months old |

Although a cat has an average life span of about 14 years, it is surprising to observe that 38% of them were small kittens.

The fact that body-parts had been included or even packaged separately, along with very young kittens being killed, led Ginsburg to suggest that the demand for properly-packaged cats must have been so great that a cat-mummification industry had probably been established, organized to sell ready-made cat-packages to the followers of the God Bastet. Seemingly, when running out of mature cats to kill, they used kittens. When that, too, was not sufficient to meet the demand, they supposedly started dismembering cats and mummified individual body-parts of cats or any other dead animal available at that moment, while giving the proper shape to the bundle so as to imitate the normal packaging.

Although Ginsburg's conclusion seems, at first sight, to be somewhat plausible, a more likely scenario was offered by Boessneck and Driesch (1987) who, in 1983, investigated galleries of ibises near Tuna-El-Gebel. They stated in their report:

*"All ages are encountered: from egg and recently-born hatchlings up to full grown adults... Many of the bodies must have laid on the ground for a period of time or had first been located some time after the death of the birds before they were mummified as foxes or other predators had the opportunity to eat them. Snails had crawled into their feathers or cockroaches lived, along with their larvae, on and in the bird's bodies."* (Translation from the German text of Boessneck and Driesch, 1987, 55)

These explanations are well-taken and supply strong support to the general concept of radioactivity permeating into a number of regions of Egypt.

The mummification (or, better said, the packaging) of these birds must have taken place quite some time after they had died, lying all over the countryside, thus affording the possibility to scavenging animals to feast on the carcasses, ripping them apart, consuming certain of the body-parts, while discarding others. And, most probably, in due course, a good many of these scavengers must also have died.

At a given point in time, the knowledgeable leaders who were aware that radioactivity had felled so many animals and birds, must have ordered their underlings to collect everything pertaining to animals and birds, no matter how insignificant and torn-apart the remnants might have been, to bundle them up in linen, and promptly bury them wherever they could. Let us remember that burial of radioactive substances is the constant policy and admonition given by our present authorities.

Layers of dirt and stones absorb radiation. The fact that these carcasses must have laid on the ground for some time is not surprising, given the enormous quantities of birds that fell dead all over the countryside. It would have taken a large contingent of laborers running through the vast expanses of the marshes or the desert to collect hundreds of thousands of dead birds, cats, dogs, etc.

We now have a cogent reason why unhatched eggs, pieces of bones, feathers, or tails of birds, etc. were all collected, "mummified" and then placed in underground depositories. This also explains why a number of cats had been strangled. There could have been a number of poor felines that probably survived but vociferously meowed in agony and pain. The collecting team of laborers might have wanted to put an end to their misery and ended their lives by twisting their necks.

When a radiation cloud invaded a region, all species of animals and birds living in that area must have died. Boessneck and Driesch's detailed report (1987, 146) supports such an expectation. They pointed out that other birds had been found to be mixed in with the ibises they investigated. All told, they named 38 different types, including 3 storks, 27 falcons, 11 sparrow-hawks, 1 coot, 3 cormorants, 3 buzzards, 2 vultures, many eagles, ravens, birds of prey, condors, 4 owls, 1 crow, etc., a list that is almost a duplication of the one given by Kessler.

If only ibises were consecrated to the God Thoth, why did the ancient Egyptians include so many other varieties of birds in their packages? They certainly knew the difference between an ibis and an eagle or an owl. Obviously, there was more to this overt "religious practice" than meets the eye. No doubt, the Egyptian population, and probably most of the lower-echelon of priests, considered that some sacred duty was involved, one that would satisfy the Gods. By doing so, they were unwittingly performing the hidden agenda of the organizers. They were the ones who collected any dead species or their parts.

Alain Charron (1989, 209-213) wrote an article in French whose title translates into "Massacres of animals at the late epoch." In it he expounds ideas that support the conclusions reached at by the present research. The following quotations have been translated:

> "... there is no other solution than to believe that the crocodiles were killed. The same goes for the ibises of Abydos, el Gebel or Roda... " (210)

> "... after domesticated animals, such as cats and dogs, or those raised, such as ibises or falcons, must have been killed at specific periods of time." (211)

> "One must suppose that they have been killed at a precise moment." (211)

> "... it ensues that all these cats were in good health at the time they were strangulated." (212)

> "It seems that these massacres started under the reign of Nectanebo II" (212) [360-343 BC; XXX-th Dynasty.]

It is interesting to note that Charron also concluded that a good portion of the deaths took place at the same time, during the same event, and not one at a time. The word "massacre" denotes a slaughter taking place during a given event, and at the same time. Such an occurrence could only take place when a radioactive cloud carries its death-laden atmosphere to a multitude of living organisms located in a given area. The vast majority of these deaths cannot be attributed to a group of people running around to kill all the birds they can encounter, provided, of course, these birds did not fly away when the gang of "killers" approached them, an unrealistic conjecture. Similar arguments can be offered for the wholesale deaths of thousands of fish, crocodiles, cats, dogs, etc.

This conclusion supports the construction of the underground tunnels and galleries to store the vast quantities of dead ibises, dogs, cats, etc. It is not logical to expect that these huge quantities of dead animals and birds were piled up on the desert sands, waiting for a crew of laborers to dig underground tombs for warehousing the dead corpses. If these laborers were using only copper or bronze chisels along with wooden mallets, it would have taken them months, if not years, to perform such a job, a waiting period that would have been unacceptable. Obviously, these tunnels must have been constructed much faster to accommodate the mountains of birds and animals. We are forced to conclude that they had a much faster means to cut into rock or to dig underground. Such an action could only have been achieved via mechanical means that could easily chew into the rock and create any type of corridors, galleries, and rooms desired.

It should be kept in mind that the almost automatic fashion in creating these animal depositories are not the only examples we encounter in ancient Egypt. Outstanding examples to be cited are: the descending passageway in Khufu's pyramid, or, the so-called well-shaft, details on which will be given in another book of the present research project.

## TIMING

The subject of animal deaths raises a very important question. When did they die? This question is important because the answer could help explain when the pyramids and temples were destroyed. From among some 118 pyramids, about 110 have been utterly destroyed in a manner that implies the application of enormous power. Since ancient Egypt seems to have manipulated radioactive substances, it is most probable that the demolition could be attributed to explosions based on atomic power, given the millions upon millions of tons of masonry that had been made to crumble while transforming them into rubble (a subject detailed in a future book in this series). It is logical to deduce that with the destruction of every structure, the atmosphere became filled with radioactive fallout that ensued, thus killing millions of birds and animals.

If C-14 tests were performed on a number of these dead species, we would be able to pinpoint their dates of death which, in turn, could signify the approximate date of the destruction of the pyramids and temples. For example, Ginsburg (1999, 189) reported that the cats he worked on, were found to belong to the Ptolemaic era (about 300 to 0 BC).

On the other hand, Minault-Gout (1983, 113-119) discovered at Balat (Oasis of Dakhla) a small tomb dating to the end of the Old Kingdom or perhaps to the beginnings of the First Intermediate Period. In it, said archaeologist found 23 buried cats. The death of these cats can be dated to about 2,200 to 2,100 BC, which means about 2,000 years earlier than those discovered by Ginsburg. This could indicate that there were at least two periods when the destruction of the pyramids might have occurred. It is certain that other waves of destruction waves took place at other times, such as, for example during Akhnaten's time (ca 1,345 BC), a fact that had been confirmed in at least one stele found in the temple of Amun at Karnak which was dated to Tutankhamun's time (ca 1,330 BC). The text had been translated by Bennett (1939, 9), part of which read:

> *"Now when his Majesty arose as king the temples of the Gods and Goddesses beginning from Elephantine to the marshes of the Delta—[had] fallen into neglect their shrines had fallen into desolation and became tracts overgrown.... plants, their sanctuaries were as if they had never been their halls were a trodden path. The land was in confusion, the Gods forsook the land."*

This text clearly tells us that at around 1330 BC all the temples had been razed and structures had been destroyed.

A word of caution has to be sounded on the dating of the deaths of animals. There seems to be a tendency among Egyptologists to connect the death and burial of animals to the date of the tomb in which they were found. In the above-mentioned example offered by Minault-Gould, 23 cats were found buried in a small tomb that had been dated to the end of the Old Kingdom — that means to about 2200 BC. However, we must not jump to the conclusion that the cats belonged to the same era. It could well be that they died some 2000 years later but were interred in the nearest available tomb that the local population could locate. Such a move would have offered them the big advantage of being located underground, thus capable of absorbing the radiation emanating from the carcasses of the dead cats. Of course, if this burial was handled by local individuals, they would not have had the slightest idea why they were asked to do as they did. They would have been given orders by those who knew exactly what was involved, and why it had to be done as performed. Or else, it had been performed by a team of those who knew.

The dating of the death of animals is exceedingly important. It would shed light and solve a great number of other problems. Such a crucial matter must be handled with all the scientific tools available to our present society, such as, for example, C-14 tests.

## HUMANS

The next logical expectation would be the death of humans. If land animals, birds, and reptiles had been contaminated, then people living in that vicinity must have been exposed to the same dosages. In such an event, death must have occurred to hundreds of individuals and not just to a few of them. A search through reports given by 19th century archaeologists confirms this expectation.

Rhind (1862, 132) submitted that *"...bodies of the humble classes were, at Thebes, deposited in large catacombs... and piled together to the number, it is said, of hundreds."*

Rouyer (1809, 214) stated (as translated from his French text), *"... one finds thousands of mummies heaped on top of each other."*

Pettigrew (1834, 40) referred to a Captain Light who *"...found thousands of dead bodies placed in horizontal layers side by side."*

Belzoni (1820, 157) pointed out that one place *"...was chocked with mummies."* He also reported *"Thus I proceeded from one cave to another also full of mummies piled in various ways."*

Wilkinson (1841, 400) pointed out that *"mummies of the lower orders were buried together in a common repository."*

Similar reports had been offered by Lortet (1905) who had discovered human packaged bundles thrown in together with those of crocodiles in a cave near Menfalut.

The fact was established that thousands of dead humans had been found amassed unceremoniously in piles in caves or other storage facilities. Wilkinson, for example, used the word "repository" and not "grave," which would suggest that these were not regular grave pits, but mass-accumulation of dead bodies. It is difficult to believe that these caves or common pits had been used each time one individual died of natural causes somewhere on the eastern shores of the Nile. It would have taken decades to mummify and bury, one by one, thousands of poor people to be thrown into a heap of corpses, inside a cave, far away from populated areas. Even if these were poor people, we must remember that indigent families love their dead just as dearly as rich people do theirs. They would have wanted to extend a decent burial to their kin. A plain pit dug in a nearby lot would have served the purpose, rather than allow the corpse to be thrown onto a heap of unknown individuals. It is not a costly matter for poor people to dig a hole in the ground and inter their beloved ones.

One gets the impression, that these "repositories" were stuffed with dead humans, placed there practically all at the same time. Such a wholesale death could well have been the result of a massive exposure to radiation within a certain region, thus leaving hardly any family member—poor or rich—to take care of the departed.

## FLORA

Since all sorts of animals, birds, reptiles, and human beings died out in ancient Egypt, the flora of that region must also have been affected at the same time. Lortet indirectly gave support to such an expectation. While reporting on a certain baboon burial ground, he included an important observation:

> "...In these coffins we often found flowers and almost always there were numerous sprouts of Balanites Egyptiaca...Their seeds had been carefully extracted with a piercing instrument as though they wanted to avoid that a living plant would sprout in an area inhabited by the dead." (Translated from the French text of Lortet 1905, 385).

Lortet was right. They did want to stop the future germination of the plants which, probably, had been exposed to radiation. They had to make sure that those plants would utterly perish and would not be ingested by future generations. Unfortunately we do not know the ensuing state of health of the individuals who manipulated the contaminated kernels.

A very similar report was submitted by Leblanc (1983, 8-9) who excavated tomb No. 58 in the Valley of the Queens. He also came across a quantity of *Balanite egyptiaca* kernels whose center parts had been scooped out, exactly as had been reported by Lortet some 80 years earlier. The picture published by Leblanc showed the hole in the center of the kernels. In addition, he pointed out that although this tree used to be very abundant in Nubia, it became rare during the Roman times. In fact, botanist A. R. Delile who had come along with the Napoleonic Expedition, reported (1824, 263-280) having found very few of these trees in the region of Assiut.

The reality is that a given species of a tree had become extinct. This aspect is further underscored by an article by Percy Newberry (in Petrie 1890, 49-50) who reported that *Balanites egyptiaca* no longer grows in Egypt. He submitted additional details about this reconfirmation of an extinct tree species:

> *"The fruit-tree which appears to have been the commonest... was the Balanites Agyptiaca, Del., a small tree, now known in Abyssinia by the Arabic name of Heglig. At the present day this tree is widely distributed in North Tropical Africa, from Senegal to Abyssinia, but it does not now occur in Egypt in the wild state. Indeed, but very few cultivated specimens are now to be found in Egypt, and these are only to be met within the gardens of the larger towns...In early times, however, the tree must have had a far wider distribution for stones of its fruits have been frequently found in the ancient tombs at Gizeh, Thebes, Dakhel, and various other sites in Lower and Upper Egypt."*

In the same article, Newberry submitted another thought-provoking example:

> *"Another fruit esteemed by the Egyptians of the XIIth dynasty was that of Dellach palm-tree (Hyphaene argun Mart.). Thirty stones of this palm were discovered at Kahun... This palm is not now grown in Egypt, and, so far as it at present known, only inhabits a few valleys of the Nubian desert within the great bed of the Nile between Korusko and Abu Hamed."*

An additional tree disappeared from the Egyptian scene, as reported by Newberry:

> *"The Mimusops schimperi, Hochst., perhaps the persea of the ancients, was also grown in Central Egypt in XIIth dynasty times, for both its fruit and leaves have been identified among the Kahun remains. At the present day it is not known in Egypt, only occurring in Central Africa and in Abyssinia."*

Other varieties of trees, such as the Dom palm:

> *"...though not uncommon in Egypt at the present day, appears (if we may judge from the numbers of its fruits which have been discovered at Kahun and elsewhere in Egypt) to have also had a wider distribution in ancient times. It was called the 'mama', and it is often mentioned in the ancient literature of Egypt."*

Why would popular varieties of trees become extinct in the territory of Egypt while others have seen their growth greatly diminish in comparison to what they used to be in ancient times? A possibly meaningful observation had been reported by Gain (1902, 269-271). He submitted the results of some studies conducted on a number of wheat and barley seeds, obtained from some of the tombs at Gebelein, Gourneh, Saqqara, Denderah, and Thebes (V, IX, XVIII, XX, and XXI dynasties respectively). The study aimed at determining whether these grains had maintained their germination capacities after having been dormant for so many millennia:

> *"...We must note that the pharaonic seeds usually have a very beautiful outer appearance. The only somewhat noteworthy exterior characteristic consists, most of the time, in a reddish brown tint....*

*It has been clearly verified that the adherence of the seed to the albumen does no longer exist. The whole embryo can be separated without any difficulty....The embryo has kept its cellular internal organization but each cell has, very obviously, undergone a chemical change, which confirms that all the seeds studied had lost their germination potential since a long time ago...All the rest of the embryo has a very pronounced reddish tint. Various microchemical reactions have been tried on the cells of these ancient embryos; they gave different results than those obtained from modern embryos—even 50 year old ones."* (Translated from the French text of Gain.)

Whether such radical changes can be attributed to radiation exposure cannot be concluded from the data of this 1902 report. However, one of Gain's remarks could be thought-provoking; he observed that all the seeds had "...a very pronounced reddish tint."

Carter (1972, 222) had reported:

*"Another interesting subject peculiar to the tomb of Tutankhamen, and one which has been a puzzle throughout our work, was the existence of a pink film (soluble in warm water) deposited over all exposed surfaces within the chambers—ceilings, floors, walls, and objects—a phenomenon so peculiar to the discovery that it appears to be part result of the humidity already discussed. This deposit prevailed everywhere; it varied in density as well as in colour —pink to bright red—in accordance with conditions, but where an object or material covered another, or where an object stood against and protected a part*

*of any surface, the deposit, if not absent, was of a*
*far lighter density, causing either behind or below*
*the object a faintly indicated impression."*

It is naturally surprising that such a "pink to a bright red" film should have covered everything in sight in that particular tomb, as well as the seeds found in some of the other burials specified by Gain.

The present chapter deals only with a few of the well-known "consecrated" animals. There were others that might have been just as "sacred" to some of the people, such as the Mnevis bull, the Apis bull or the Buchis bull. A detailed study of the various bulls respected within the Egyptian society would constitute a very extensive project in itself, one that will be taken up in a subsequent volume of the present study.

# CHAPTER FIVE

# UNDERGROUND FIRES

*"But how comes it that it is so hot amongst the mummies? It seems as if there were fires burning in some oven close by... the heat is suffocating." (Loti, La mort de Philae, 1909)*

If our theory of the use of radioactive substances in ancient Egyptian tombs is correct, then the tombs should have displayed an important tell-tale clue: high heat.

The surprising observations made by archaeologists confirm that, indeed, a large number of such tombs had certainly been destroyed by "fires" or exposed to searing heat. The record is full of such examples.

At this point it is well to define two terms:

A- FIRE: The burning of combustible materials, such as wood, in the presence of ample oxygen, i.e. air , which would be accompanied by flames. The residue would be ashes.

B - CHARCOAL: Exposure of wood to an intensive source of heat within a tightly sealed compartment from which air (i.e. oxygen) was excluded. The residue would be charcoal.

The physical presence of ashes or charcoal forewarn us that:

A- The ashes should indicate to us that full combustion had taken place in the presence of air, accompanied by flames.

B- Ashes (or ash-like powders) could also be the result of vegetable matter having been seared by very high heat without air being present; said substance would have charred or carbonized.

C- The presence of charcoal proves that wood had been exposed to very high heat, but in the absence of air, that must have been generated from within the enclosure.

Archaeologists working in the ruins of earlier tombs and mastabas were almost always confronted with a puzzling problem. They found charcoal, ashes and carbonized remnants, which indicated that there must have been extreme heat generated within those underground chambers and magazines. A rereading of a few reports published by them will illustrate and clarify the extent of the problems surrounding these occurrences. To understand these situations, we have to review the basic construction technique applied by the ancient Egyptians when creating the pre-dynastic and early dynastic tombs.

They first dug a pit in the ground, whose size differed greatly, depending upon the project. The four sides and internal separations were made of mud-bricks. Normally, one would have expected that such burials would have been properly served and protected if the surrounding walls had been built with a single layer of bricks, extending a thickness of about 12 inches. Instead, archaeologists were surprised to find thicknesses of 3 to 16 feet. Such massive enclosure walls were always enigmatic.

This depression in the ground was then divided into independent roomettes by the insertion of other thick walls. However, in most cases, such cells were not connected to each other. The only means to access them would have been through the roof, at the time of construction. In some other instances they built several individual roomettes all around the main pit, again, with no interconnection between them, thus creating insulated spaces. The tombs of kings Zet, Zer, and Merneith are good examples of such structures. In other instances, they built a whole array of cubicles, as shown in the case of the tomb at Umm-el–Kab.

The floors were usually either paved with a single layer of brick or were covered by wooden planks; sometimes they displayed only gravel and sand. The ceilings were normally built with round wooden beams about 12 inches in diameter supporting a variety of overlaid materials, such as wooden planks (some about 24 inches wide and 5 inches thick}, straw, branches of trees, pebbles, or any other filling materials the builders happened to have had on hand. The planks and beams were usually anchored into the walls .In effect, most of these earlier mastaba magazines turned out to be almost airtight, underground boxes with thick walls.

At the very outset of these discoveries, these unusual features should have warned Egyptologists that something out of the ordinary was involved with these large burial grounds. Two interesting observations should be underscored:

(A) In most cases, no human bones were found. Instead most of the main rooms and satellite cubicles were filled with jars. Occasionally, a skeleton was discovered in some of the outlying roomettes. This situation would indicate, that to start with, no corpse had been inserted in the tomb, but only jars filled with mud. Obviously, one gets the impression that these large structures had not been erected to bury a human being but instead hundreds of jars. At times, a corpse might have been inserted, if available at the moment when the tomb had to be closed.

(B) The black mud-bricks must have been exposed to such an intense heat that they baked red. This observation had been repeated many times by archaeologists who had been active in various other mastabas.

A typical example of conditions found in these underground installations was provided by Emery in his report on tomb 3471, excavated at Saqqara. He dated it to the reign of Zer, who ruled during the early part of the First Dynasty (ca 3,000 BC). This structure displayed two tiers of magazines. Theoretically, a human being was supposed to have been buried in the main chamber. Yet, Emery (1949, 17-18) submitted the following important observations when he realized that this tomb had been ravaged by fire:

> "Room O ...The burial chamber... it is probable that the fire started in this room and it has suffered to a greater extent than any other part of the tomb. Apart from the burnt fragments of numerous stone vessels, nothing survived but the charred corner of what appeared to be a gigantic wooden coffin (Cat. No. 549) and the remains of a large wooden bier with copper fittings (Cat. No. 539) which had been placed inside it and on which the body of the owner had probably been laid. We found no trace of anatomical material; undoubtedly this had been destroyed by the fire which had been so intense that the mudbrick wall of the room had been baked red.
>
> "Room E...Charred fragments of furniture, probably parts of a bed...
>
> "Room K...42 large wine jars ...stacked in two layers. Most of these jars were complete with their mud sealings, but unfortunately they were so damaged by fire that the seal impressions were mostly destroyed.

*"Room S...Below these fragments we found a series of stone bowls laid face downwards, on top of each other with the charred remains of layers of cloth between each vessel...The removal of these objects disclosed the burnt remains of fine basket-work boxes."*

If room "O" did not contain any "anatomical material," it meant that no corpse had been placed in that room. Even if a fire had raged and consumed that space, charred bones or small fragments should have been found. Emery's (1954) report on his excavations at tomb 3503, depicted a similar picture of intense fire having consumed most of the contents of the magazines:

*"Room J ...This room was almost entirely burnt out and until about 1.00 metre above floor level was filled with the clean sand rubble filling which had fallen in from the magazine above when the roof collapsed. Below the strata of burnt wood from the roof we found the fragments of pottery vessels...*

*"Room K...This room is almost entirely filled with clean debris from the filling of the magazine above it. Below the strata of burnt roofing the room contained nothing beyond fragments of pottery...*

*"Room L...The burial chamber ...The height of the clean debris above the burnt strata of 1.50 metres shows a wealth of material which must have existed in this room before the fire almost totally destroyed it. The charred remains of a big wooden sarcophagus could be traced on the stone floor of the tomb. As far as could be ascertained, it measured approximately 2.70 metres by 1.80 metres...On the remains of the wooden flooring of this sarcophagus we found*

*a few fragile human remains, the sex of which is uncertain, and some fragments of gold foil..."*

In this particular case, Emery did find some human remains, an indication that a corpse had been placed in that chamber. The fact that the burnt strata had a depth of about 5 feet indicates that a large amount of wood had been present in that chamber, and that a very intense heat must have existed to completely char such a mass of wooden objects. Of course, Emery is using the term "char" in a more generic way. Given the conditions found in those rooms, it is certain that he was referring to charcoal.

It is worth observing that in all these cases of "fires," jars are found in the areas afflicted.

Sayce and Clarke (1905, 257-262) excavated at El-Kab, an area where predynastic or Old Kingdom tombs must have existed underneath the newer XIIth dynasty (ca 2,000 to 1,775 BC) structures. They dug pits and trenches in various places and almost always reached layers of charcoal. Their associate, F.W. Green, reported some of these finds:

> *"At a distance of 0.30 m. below the stones is a thin stratum of charcoal representing the Old Kingdom level of the ground*
>
> *"...4 metres below the present surface, on a thin stratum discoloured by charcoal...*
>
> *"...The stratum that has accumulated... is discoloured with charcoal and contains many fragments of pottery...*
>
> *"Trench No. 13... the earth blackened by charcoal... This bed of dark earth must have been of considerable thickness at one time as, even in the depression, it is as much as 4 metres thick. [about 13 ft].*

*"...below the top of the NW corner stone, a stratum 0.10 m. thick was found composed of wood ashes, charcoal and occasional pieces of pottery.*

*"...at 0.90 m. lower down was found a thick stratified band of charcoal-discoloured earth, which ...is 0.30 m. thick ...Pit No. 8 shewed much the same characteristics...*

*A pit No. 15 was sunk ...where a well-defined charcoal-discoloured stratum is met, containing Old Kingdom pottery...another dense band of charcoal-discoloured each is reached, reddened in patches by hearths...Below this second stratum is a third, chiefly composed of broken Old Kingdom rough pottery and large pieces of charcoal..."*

Once again we observe that jars/pottery go hand in hand with charcoal. The above quotations depict the picture of an ancient series of tombs that once had existed at that site. We claim that a number of ancient mastabas with wooden interiors or ceilings had been storing jars with radioactive substances. The wooden pieces turned into charcoal, the ceilings caved in and the entire tomb became smothered under the weight of rubble, stones, and sand. A number of centuries thereafter, another group of people built their edifices on top of the tomb. Petrie (1901A, 2) gave us interesting details of another ancient tomb that was originally excavated by Amelineau, a French archaeologist:

*"...the most interesting remains of the wooden chamber of Zer, a carbonized mass 28 feet by 3 feet, studded with copper fastenings, have entirely disappeared, and of another tomb we read" " j'y recontrai environ deux cents kilos de charbon de bois" (Fouilles 1896, p.15) which has been all removed."*

The statement of Amelineau translated: "I encountered about 200 kilos of charcoal." Such an amount of about 440 pounds of charcoal, located in one grave, is a very impressive quantity. It indicates that a large amount of wood had been exposed to a very potent heat, which, in turn, indicates radioactivity had been present.

Petrie (1913, 15) also reported on mastaba No. 1060 found in Tarkhan, located between those of Zer and Meneith and dated to the First Dynasty's times:

> "...However from the numerous large-sized pieces of charcoal also found everywhere in the central chamber, there must have been a great quantity of woodwork used. The only vestige of this still in situ is the charred end of a beam still in the hole 3 inches below the level of the roof-ledge..."

Petrie's associate Wainwright, reported on the vases found in a certain grave:

> "They had almost all been blackened by the burning, and most of them contained what appeared to be the charred remains of scented fat, so common at this period. None of them contained ashes so often found in the alabasters in the small graves of the same date in this cemetery ...Many alabasters were considerably corroded inside, as if by long use with some slightly acid substance." (Wainwright, in Petrie 1913A, 18).

In another of his publications, Emery stated:

> "...This destruction ...was caused by ancient plunderers who perhaps by accident set the tomb on fire, thus causing the collapse of the wooden roof which, with the fire, completely destroyed the contents of all but three of the chambers ...The partly burnt fragments of numerous vessels of alabaster,

*basalt, and schist. ...the fire, which had been so intense that the mud brick walls of the chamber had been baked red..." (Emery 1939, 427)*

*"The tomb was first plundered shortly after burial, by tunneling below the superstructure. To cover the evidence of their sacrilege, the robbers appear to have deliberately fired the burial chamber which, in the confined space without any outlet, smoldered for weeks and, with the ultimate destruction of the wooden roofing, caused the collapse of the middle of the vast structure with its magazines and rubble filling .This firing of the burial chamber after plundering is a common feature and has been noted in other large tombs of the period at Saqqara , Abydos, and Naqadah." (Emery 1954, 5).*

The facts noted are naturally thought-provoking, although the explanation submitted is most unlikely and theoretical, once we understand the accompanying effects of radioactivity. There are two aspects that stand out in the various reports offered by all the past archaeologists who excavated Egyptian underground tombs. The earlier ones display the traces of previous fires, while most of them indicate that "thieves" had broken in and started fires. The notion that "robbers" plundered each one of the hundreds of individually separated magazines, and then set fires to each one of them, is far-fetched. Such a suggestion is not realistic as fires in underground air-tight areas cannot be sustained without the presence of an abundance of air. A thief who is interested in stealing valuables would dig a shaft or tunnel into the underground rooms, collect whatever it is he was interested in and run. Thieves are hardly worried about the sacrilege of breaking in. If they were, they would not have broken into the tomb, to start with. They would not need to cover their traces, not when their actions was taking place in the middle of an empty desert.

Our explanation to this problem is evident. Jars of radioactive substances, inserted in each one of the underground storage-rooms, would emit a very substantial amount of heat on a continuous basis (besides the radiation). Had oxygen been abundant in that spot, wood would have burst into flames and burnt to ashes. Without adequate supply of oxygen, vegetable matter would carbonize, wood would turn into charcoal, clay would fuse and bricks would bake. All of these effects are present in the ruins of underground chambers in ancient Egypt. Of cause, earlier archaeologists cannot be blamed for the untenable explanations they gave during their time when radioactivity was unknown.

The wooden roofs provide an interesting hint on how these builders used the effects of radioactivity to make their task easier and safer. Instead of digging shafts into the ground, which would have been a more difficult job, they simply created a pit in the sand and finished it as an enclosure with wooden ceilings within which they then deposited quantities of jars filled with their usual mud-mixtures. This type of construction was a premeditated act. They knew and expected the roof to self-destruct. When the wood beams finally disintegrated because of exposure to the intensive heat generated within the chamber, the ceiling would have caved in. All the gravel, sand, and other materials they had heaped on top of the ceiling, would then cascade down on the stored jars and smother them. Thus, instead of continuing to maintain an orderly, room they would have ended up as piles of rubble on top of the jars.

As a natural result of desert winds, the place would soon be overblown with sand, creating new dunes among similar natural dunes in the desert. These montecules would not particularly attract attention of future scavengers; the result would have been an effort-less, safe, burial ground for radioactive material in the empty desert.

Are these destroyed mastabas still radioactive? This question cannot be answered with any degree of accuracy, as it depends completely upon a number of factors, including the type of substance originally used, its concentration within the lethal mixture, the time elapsed, and so on. Although Emery did consider that thieves had broken in into the mastabas he excavated, he also submitted some very thoughtful observations. When analyzing his findings in tomb 3503 at Saqqara, he stated:

> "...The plundering which must have taken place at no great period after the burial, was accomplished by driving a tunnel, approximately 1.00 metre wide and 0.70 metre high, below ground level... In the mouth of the shaft and on the shelf around it we found a large number of jar sealings with their impressions well preserved... This was a fortunate, if puzzling discovery, for the sealings recovered from the rooms of the substructure were so badly burnt that little remained of the inscriptions. The presence of jar sealings at the head of the plunderer's entrance cannot be explained, for no remains of the pottery jars to which they belonged were found with them, and even so, wine-jars can hardly be considered the usual plunder of grave robbers." (Emery 1954, 139).

His logical conclusion is correct, as far as it goes; yet, it has to be interpreted in a different manner. Grave robbers were not the ones who broke in. It probably was the same group of organizers, or one affiliated with them, who had been in a hurry to temporarily bury their available lethal substances which they now wanted to retrieve. It must be kept in mind that the reentry action did not occur only in mastabas. We witnessed the same activity taking place in shaft-tombs, and even in certain pyramids.

Bruyere (1934 A, 95) reported on tomb 2001 which he had excavated at Deir-El-Medineh. A slanted ramp led to a square room that contained a vertical shaft dug into its floor. The shaft measured about 10 by 10 feet and extended to a depth of about 45 feet, at the bottom of which was a large room, about 50 by 16 feet. All around the room, niches containing sarcophagi had been hewn into the rock (Fig. 24). The entire floor was covered by a 7 feet thick layer of lithic debris in which were found some human bones and fragments of blackened mummies. Eleven granite or limestone sarcophagi were found. Most of the covers had been thrown off or broken. Almost all sarcophagi had been emptied out previously, at some unknown date.

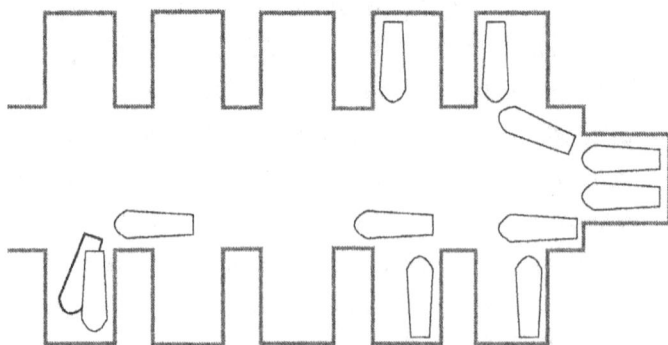

Fig. 24   Tomb 2001 at Deir el Medineh, as reported by Bruyere (1934, Fig. 62)

Everywhere existed traces of a "violent fire" which could be seen on the ceilings, the walls, the shaft, and even in the square room at the top of the shaft.

Mastabas were not the only burials that had been exposed to "violent fires"; although shaft tombs were usually erected after the era of the earlier burials. They too continued to be "burnt."

It is significant to note that the same debris due to "violent fires" was also found in the North Ibis Catacomb at Saqqara, as reported by Nicholson (1995, 8):

> "The catacomb is, in places, heavily chocked with debris comprising broken pottery and rubble, and the walls are often smoke-blackened, apparently from past conflagrations within the galleries... So intense were some of these fires that mud-bricks became fired in situ."

150

J.M.Wainwright (1852, 157-8) made a similar observation after his visit to the Saqqara area:

*"There are in the neighborhood many cat and ibis mummy pits, in addition to the human ones, but we only visited one of the cat-pits ....*

*...After descending gradually in this manner for some distance, we came to heaps of broken vases of rough earthenware of a red color, which had formerly contained cat-mummies... we soon were enabled to see where the mummy pots had been as yet undisturbed, They were piled one upon another ... but how far or how deep they extended we could not tell, for the excavated rock was filled with them to the very top ... generally speaking the mummies are reduced to a black powder, and the linen envelopes are completely rotten ...*

*... we made our escape from this curious but disgusting place ... All around us were numerous other mummy-pits which had been emptied of their contents."*

The statement that most stands out is that the "mummies are reduced to black powder", a tell-tale sign for the exposure to a constant emission of intensive heat which, in the absence of oxygen, consumed the cats' bodies by charring them.

The same observation was made by Nicholson, Jackson, and Frazer (1999, 214):

*"In 1995 however, a gallery (designated as 24) was discovered in which all the mummies were buried without pots...Rather the birds are stacked in neat rows right across the gallery, and to a considerable depth. All are black and extremely friable. Where they have been examined all are of ibis, rather than substitutes of any kind."*

Ibises are white. For them to have turned "black and extremely friable" means that they, too, had been exposed to a continuous stream of searing heat before or after they had been deposited in those galleries. In this particular case, we could consider that not only were the birds killed by exposure to radioactivity, but they might have been stacked in rooms where jars of radioactive substances had been stored. These unfortunate birds had been exposed to a double dose of destructive elements.

Previously, reference had been made to a catacomb of animals that Petrie (1900, 28-30) had located in Denderah, "...which were begun in the XVIIIth Dynasty, and were added to until Roman times." Surprisingly, he had encountered heaps of burnt bones in some of the underground chambers, which, according to him, was an indication that a fierce fire had raged. Amid these burnt bones, Petrie found "...pieces of blue glazed ware," which were equally burnt "...so that not much of the blue survives." In fact, "...most of the surface is reduced to metallic copper by the action of the muffled fire." The conflagration must have been so fierce that "... the whole inside of the passage and chamber is vitrified and the slag has run down the walls. This reduced the bulk to a layer of merely calcified bones."

The type of effects described by Petrie suggested the past existence of an enormous amount of heat. He had also pointed out that not all rooms, located adjacent to each other, displayed the same signs of infernal fire. The latter did not touch the chambers of the hawks, nor some of the other chambers. Had it been a normal fire, it is logical to expect that it would have engulfed the whole underground area. Petrie tried to hypothesize about the cause that had created such fires:

> *"What was the cause of this burning? At first we thought it might have been intentional, but there is no reason to suppose so. Rather, it seems, the chambers had been filled with animal mummies, wrapped in cloth*

152

*with resins to preserve them; such mummies had also
been stacked in the narrow passage until it was filled,
and mingled with them were pieces of broken furniture
from the temple. Then, by some accident the mass
caught fire... the use of these catacombs belongs then
to the earlier half of the XVIII th Dynasty. There is no
evidence as to when the burning took place, except that
it was before Roman times." (Petrie 1900, 29)*

Not knowing the very existence of radioactivity, Petrie was forced
to conclude that "some accident" must have occurred, which meant
that he did not know why such "fires" had started. We should note,
however, that he is dating the catacomb to the 18-th Dynasty, about a
thousand years or more before the Roman occupation of Egypt.

Another piece of evidence had been offered by de Morgan
(1897, 154) while excavating tombs in the vicinity of Nagada at
a tel measuring about 200 by 235 feet. It proved to be an ancient
mastaba-type burial. The bricks surrounding it:

*" ...were reddened by fire... It was not the type of
heat traces observed in fired bricks; instead it was
that of an intense fire that had engulfed the entire
structure. Twenty-one chambers were discovered
....none of which had been robbed in ancient times,
but a fire of extreme violence, lit intentionally, had
consumed most of the objects..."* (Translated from
French text of de Morgan.)

Despite this devastation, de Morgan was able to piece together
more than 300 large jars along with a quantity of hard stone vases.
He considered that this grave went back to the times of the First
Dynasty. (ca 3,000 BC).

Another important example was offered by G.Wainwright
who excavated the mastaba near the Meidum pyramid, known as
the Great Mastaba No. 17. He discovered that this tomb had no

longer an entrance leading from the outside, as it had been sealed off by tightly plugging the entrance corridor with heavy, squared blocks. In essence, it had been turned into an isolated underground chamber with no interconnection to the outside world. The burial chamber contained a sarcophagus that had been previously opened by the proverbial "thieves". Nothing was found in the vat, while the room was, as usual, in shambles. Wainwright's additional details are revealing and confirm an ongoing pattern:

> *"...[the thief]...knew exactly the position of the chamber, and tunneling from the south end for about 20 yards from the point nearest to the construction, he made straight for the end of the long north and south passage, which he struck unerringly, and forcing out one stone, apparently by means of a charcoal fire, he entered...We found a large quantity of charcoal against the outside of the wall...and the stones in the immediate neighborhood all bore clear traces of fire, being scorched pink and grey. There were also a few bricks piled up against the outside of the wall, all burnt red on the side facing the tunnel.*

> *"...Unfortunately the thieves had scattered everything; all the vases except one big one, were lying in the ...passage*

> *"...In front of the coffin were lying many fragments of gold foil..." (Wainwright 1910, 14).*

Once again, there is the surprised observation that "thieves" knew exactly the position of the chamber within that huge mound and burrowed along the shortest path that would lead to it. Logically it would mean that these "thieves" either had instruments to guide them in locating a radioactive source (stashed in the burial chamber), or else they were part of the original builders and had on hand the layout plans to guide them.

And, once again, we are faced with large quantities of charcoal, burnt-red bricks and stones that display the results of having been exposed to fire. At the same time we are reminded of the same type of scattering of "everything" in the burial chamber, just as had been the case in Tutankhamun's case some 1,000 years later.

Emery (1958, v3, 11) referred to a tomb located south of No. 3504, when he stated:

> *"A very large percentage of the great tombs of the First Dynasty at Sakkara, Abydos, and Nagadah have been burnt...In the present case the fire not only burnt out the burial chamber but it destroyed large areas of the superstructure to such an extent that the brickwork of walls 5 metres [ca 16.5 feet] thick was burnt red throughout. Such a fire must have smouldered for weeks and we may not be in error in considering that it was done deliberately with official sanction."*

The choice of words and descriptions of Emery are well taken. For a 16.5 feet thick mud-brick wall to burn red, through and through, implies an exposure to an enormous amount of heat applied in a continuous manner. Such a steady supply of high heat can hardly be assigned to a fire, in the true sense of the word. Naturally, for Emery, the source of such intense heat could only have been a burning fire, raging underground for weeks or months on end, a physical impossibility given that the tightly enclosed subterranean area could not have contained enough oxygen to sustain regular combustion for an extended amount of time.

The conditions encountered by other archaeologists were basically identical. These findings could be multiplied a number of times. They would be a repetition of the same observations: jars (some broken, some not), charcoal, ashes, bricks that turned red, or were even vitrified. The true reasons for these previously misunderstood effects are now becoming clear.

The quantities of jars placed in those tombs should not be minimized. Emery (1954, 3) reported that only in tomb 3504 did he find about 1,500 pieces of stone and 2,500 pieces of pottery vessels. Additionally, there could have been untold quantities that had been taken away by the "thieves."

Another aspect should be kept in mind. Not all chambers displayed the effect of fires. At times, a certain room was found to be completely destroyed by "fire", while the adjacent one, which was usually separated by a thick brick-wall, turned out to be untouched. A typical example was given by Daressy (1905, 99 - 106) who excavated ancient mastabas around the Gizeh area. At Nezlet Batran, located about 1.5 miles south of the Great Pyramid, he discovered a tomb with five chambers. Daressy reported:

> "...A fire ravaged all items made of wood and chunks of charcoal were found, having originated from the ceiling; the bricks were burnt, calcified at places, because the intensity of the fire had not been the same throughout the edifice. While certain wall panels hardly show any traces of this accident, other portions offer no consistency at all...

> "...In the large chamber "C" were found a great many jars, as well as sealings...Almost all vases were broken...At the bottom of some of them adhered a blackish substance, compact, and resembling bitumen... No traces of human skeleton were found, however in the reinforcements of the north wall, calcified cattle bones were located... The rooms "A" and "B" had a width of 2.60 m and 2.71 m respectively. [8.5 by 8.8 feet] The separating wall had a thickness of 1.18 m [3.8 feet]. The traces of fire are also visible...

*...”D” and “E”, to the north of the main chamber... are separated by a wall of 3.5 feet thickness. No fire occurred here.”*

(Translated from the French text of Daressy, 1905,101, 103)

Daressy considered this structure to date to the Old Kingdom's times. The presence of such large quantities of jars is normal and to be expected since the radioactive substances had to be carried and stored in receptacles, as was the case in most of the other so-called tombs. No human remains were encountered, hinting that this tomb actually had been constructed to store radioactive materials, and not humans. In this particular case we understand that some of the jars displayed residues of black tar, which had been used as a binder instead of the more common mud mixtures that are found in the vast majority of the jars.

Other examples were cited by Petrie (1901A, 7-11) when reporting on his findings at the necropolis of Abydos:

*“...The oldest tomb that we can definitely assign is that marked B-7...the tomb of King Ka... [20 by 10 feet]. ..The thickness of the brick walls is that of the length of one brick, about 11 inches... The chamber has never been burnt...*

*“...The tomb B-9 is perhaps that of King Zeser, who seems to have been a successor of Ka...It never was burnt.*

*“...The tomb B-10 appears to be the oldest of the great tombs ...The brick walls are 5 feet thick at the end, and 7 feet on the long side... The size is about 26 feet by 16 feet, and the depth 10.5 feet...This tomb was never burnt.*

*“...The tomb B-15 is probably that of King Sma... 26 by 16 feet... Depth 13.5 feet. This chamber was burnt.*

*"...[Re: tomb of King Zer-Ta]. ..the tomb chamber
has been built of wood ...the cast of the grain of the
wood can be seen on the mud mortar adhering to the
bricks... the walls are burnt red by the burning of
the tomb ...at the head of this stair we found several
jars ...remaining perfect, with carbonized cloth..."*

The above descriptions repeat most of the findings made by other archaeologists. The important fact is that these burnings continued over thousands of years.

We cannot conclude that all tombs containing radioactive substances must have been burnt. A number of factors would be involved, especially the concentration within the binding agent that had been used, such as bitumen, resin, or mud. A good example would be Tutankhamun's tomb. Although it had contained some lethal mixtures stored in jars, the chamber did not burn down. Some of the possible reasons might be:

A- The concentration of radioactive materials within the viscous substance found at the bottom of the jars was not great enough to create exceedingly high temperatures in the room.

B- The reentry into the tomb to extricate the lethal items and take them away, might have occurred soon after the original insertion into the chambers, thus not enough time had elapsed to generate sufficient heat to accumulate in the room.

C- Nevertheless, even under either of those two possibilities, the radiation that continued to escape from the small residue found at the bottom of the jars had been sufficient enough to be lethal to some of the archaeologists who entered the newly-opened premises, after some 3,200 years.

It should be kept in mind that the original "intruders" expected additional radiation to be given off within the chamber, even after they extracted the dangerous substance from it. They had been very careful to fill their entry-spots and entrance corridors with stones, thus making sure that enough rubble filled empty spaces to absorb further radiation coming from the rooms – a correct procedure as a deterrent and safety precaution.

This aspect was encountered in a number of underground burial-chambers. They shoveled into those rooms quantities of lithic rubble to fill up the space with stone fragments, being a substance that would absorb radiation. Examples are illustrated in Figs. 25 & 26, depicting the situations encountered by Davis.

Fig. 25    Conditions as found in room behind Golden Hall of
Harmhabi's Tomb (ca 1300 BC)

159

Fig. 26    Two views of some of the rooms within the tombs of Harmhabi and
Tut, showing quantities of rubble that had been introduced from the outside.

In other cases, they filled up the entrance door-opening with stone blocks and, at times, even plastered the area, thus completely isolating the rooms in questions. In cases such as this one, the purpose was not mainly to make it difficult for "thieves" to enter the devastated chamber, but for radiation not to leave the room. Instead, it would have been absorbed by the stones located within the chamber. The same procedure had been applied in some of the royal tombs in the Valley of the Kings as well as in the large rooms of the Serapeum where the Apis bulls were supposed to have been buried.

It is a fact that archaeologists found an unbearable heat within tombs.

For example, Charles Breasted (1923, 439), referring to Tutankhamun's chambers, observed:

> "...the heat of the tomb chambers was such that after only a brief stay in them one came forth dripping in perspiration."

Other visitors had similar experiences. Leca (1981, 258) related the searing heat found and experienced by a Mr. Jomad, a member of the Napoleonic Expeditionary Force to Egypt, during the early 1800s, who considered that a suffocating heat prevailed in the tombs he had visited at that time. Pierre Loti, the famous French author, had toured Egypt early in the 20th century. In his book, *La mort de Philae* (1909), he relates having visited the tomb of Amenhotep II (KV35) and observed:

> "But how comes it that it is so hot amongst the mummies? It seems as if there were fires burning in some oven close by...the heat is suffocating."

These and other similar experiences made by others indicate that ancient tombs still seem to be unusually hot.

Many other additional examples of underground tombs with elevated temperatures suggest that radioactivity is still present in them, even after thousands of years. Such an aspect is normal given the nature of chain reactions and half-life characteristics. Emission of heat is part of the nuclear decaying process, an aspect that can continue for future decades.

Leclant (1992) excavated a pre-dynastic grave at Minshat Abou Omar. It only contained a quantity of jars but no corpse. Some of the jars were whitish in color, while all the rest were thoroughly blackened. Perhaps, this might indicate that the latter might have contained radioactive substances which burnt the jars, while the former had been filled with inert mud, or something harmless.

Tombs were not the only place where lethal substances were stored or handled. Above ground structures were also involved in those special activities. For example, a great many jars had been found in the brick building next to the Valley Temple of the Bent pyramid. An additional confirmation was given by Reisner (1931, 238) in connection with his work at the Valley Temple of Menkaure's pyramid:

> "Small bits of charcoal were found in many rooms of Mycerinus Valley Temple but the only significant occurrence was in two magazines of the pyramid temple... A double handful of charcoal was found on the floor of the pyramid temple magazine (17) and about twice that amount scattered over the floor of (18)."

An equivalent discovery was made by Rowe (1931, 29) who reported his findings within and next to the small "chapel" (if one can call it that) adjacent to the Meidum pyramid:

> "Between a point a little to the east of the temple door and the west side of the rock dip was a thick layer of black charcoal dust containing many pieces of burnt wood, several fragments of bowls and dishes all of crude red ware with black center and all blackened by fire."

*As for the interior of that small room, Rowe pointed*
*out that "...its ceiling are considerably blackened in*
*places as if by smoke ....doorway into the courtyard,*
*which we found much smoked."*

Given the evidence we encountered till now, we claim that radioactive substances had been stored or handled in that small room, creating blackened walls and ceiling, a tell-tale sign for very high heat generated within a confined space.

Even mastabas located in out-of-way sites did not escape the policy of storing or manipulating jars with mud within their chambers. Archaeologist Minault-Gout (1992, 40-44) dug at the mastaba of Ima Pepi, situated in the necropolis of Qila-El-Dabba in the oasis of Dahkla. She reported having found two levels of constructions. In the lower level were 68 vases in the corridor plus 27 large jars leaning against the walls, while 43 sealings were dispersed on the floor. In the burial chamber everything had been thrown around, crushed, and burnt. On the floor, carbonized wooden planks were mixed in with other objects. A burnt skeleton was found in the sarcophagus.

*"A great portion of this first level had been burned*
*at the same time as the fire that raged in the*
*sarcophagus. The skeleton of black or gray bones*
*was surrounded by ashes and carbonized objects ...*
*Carbonized wooden planks (the largest being 60 x*
*15 cm) were leaning against it as well as a dense*
*mass of greasy and powdery material (37 cm wide*
*by 6 cm thick)..."*

(Translated from French text of Minault-Gout 1992, 43).

Each aspect of these descriptions suggest that the presence of radioactive substances are the culprits for the carbonization, the ashes and the fires. This report introduces a new element, "fires" within the sarcophagus itself that burnt the skeleton and any object next to it. We are forced to consider that the sarcophagus had also been used as a repository for lethal substances. Naturally, the possibility exists that, besides storing it, the organizers might have been using those materials for the production of "something".

The type of fires reported up to this point occurred mainly in the underground chambers of the earlier mastabas and shaft tombs.

As time went on, wood, as a building material, was replaced by slabs of limestone and granite. Additionally, the tombs were dug deeper into bedrock. Despite the fact that jars filled with mud continued to be inserted into these new installations, we encounter different degrees of conflagrations. Such situations can be assigned to the concentration of the "hot" substance within the mud mixture. Archaeologists continued to report having located tell-tale signs of "fires" that took place in these subterranean chambers.

Various examples have been published by many other Egyptologists. Typical examples of burial chambers were given by Wesenberg (1991) who displayed views of two subterranean tombs in the area of Medinet Habu. Both depict intensely blackened areas of walls and ceilings, conditions that must have been created by exposure to intense heat or sustained fires.

Dziobek (1994, Figs 9, 10, 11, 14, 15) published a whole series of photographs of the underground rooms of an individual named User-Amun. The conditions depicted clearly indicate the degree to which the walls of this tomb had been affected. We observe that the completely blackened areas can be found towards the ceiling. It is difficult to conceive that a fire, confined within the four walls of an underground chamber, could have raged out of control for a sustained period of time, in an ambiance with very limited amount of oxygen— if at all. Without it, flames could not have continued to burn to such an extent that they completely blackened the walls and ceiling.

Another excellent example was given by archaeologist Eigner (1984, Plt 48c) who had excavated tomb TT33. As shown in Fig.27, he found a large burial chamber that displayed blackened walls, ceiling and floors.

Fig. 27    Burial chamber of Pedamenope Tomb (TT33). Walls, ceiling, and
floor are blackened, displaying evidence of a past intensive fire.

When properly analyzed, one must conclude that some of
these examples (and many more similar ones) are not the result of
prolonged raging fires.

We have to consider that storage of radioactive substances
could emit very intensive heat that would sear anything in their
path. Of course, since such possibilities had never been considered
by archaeologists, they were inclined to attribute all of these aspects
as being the work of the proverbial "thieves" that were covering up
their traces.

Davies (1920, 2 - 5) excavated at the tomb of Antefoker, vizier
to Senwosret I (ca 1,950 BC). He reported:

> " ...The only remains of any value were the numerous
> fragments of a seated statue of Senet, over life-size,
> beautifully worked in hard limestone and painted ...
> The statue had been so broken up by violence or by
> fire that nothing was left but four or five heavy and
> formless masses, with patches of sculptured surface,
> and a quantity of flakes and fragments."

165

*" ... A problem set up by a conflagration, clearly deliberate, which has raged in the tomb, as in many another ..."*

*" ... It confined the fire to the shrine, the recesses.... the west end of the gallery, and the upper parts of the gallery near the heap, along with the heat or flame streamed outwards ... The statue was intact and either upright or fallen forward, on its face, for the whole of it is burnt ..."*

*"... nor are charred remains found as a rule ..."*

*" ... The effect of the fire has been to change all yellows to a red rather lighter than the true red, all greens to a dark slate, the blues to much the same tone, and to consume all the blacks completely, or almost so ..."*

*" ... The action of the fire extends beyond the debris in the gallery at the top of the walls, but lessens rapidly as one approaches the entrance. All the straw being burnt out of the plaster in the Shrine it is left very tender..."*

All of Davies' observations could be attributed to fires and heat. In turn all of these can be related to the existence of radioactive substances in those underground installations. They would have generated an enormous amount of heat without accompanying flames, since the supply of oxygen would be very limited in such underground chambers.

We have an additional report from the French archaeologist Bruyere who, in the early 1920s, dug up a number of tombs in the area of Deir-El-Medineh. He reported (1925, 24-26) having constantly encountered burnt premises in most of the ones he worked on. Those that had not been burnt were reported by him to have been the exception. Bruyere concluded that the fires that had raged in those underground cavities of tombs, mastabas, and burial chambers could have been the result of a systematic action undertaken by people unknown. He submitted examples, of which one will be reported here.

Mastaba 290-291 was composed of a chamber with two vertical shafts leading to seven underground chambers. Three chambers on the south side were completely burnt, while the other four rooms, on the north side, were not. Of course, to Bruyere, in the 1920s, such an anomaly was most surprising and led him to surmise all sorts of reasons as to why "thieves" would have acted in such a manner. Naturally, one of his conclusions alluded to "thieves" wanting to cover up their actions!

During the era of the 1920s, there would have been no way that he or anybody else could have known that rooms containing radioactive substances would have radiated an enormous amount of heat that would have burnt everything within those rooms, while the next chamber, separated from the first ones by thick walls, could have survived without having been incinerated. The stone walls would have absorbed both the radiation and heat waves.

Bruyere's examples were no different than those encountered by all the other archaeologists who had dug in underground chambers, tombs, mastabas, etc. While each one of them considered the culprits to have been "thieves", our modern science has given us a sound reason for thinking differently. In fact, it is time that we exonerate those poor, maligned culprits for arson they did not commit. Nor could they have done so even if they wanted to. (This does not mean to say that there was no bonafide thievery going on in olden days.)

Instead, we must lay the blame where it belongs: on the assorted teams who had used ancient Egypt as a burial ground for radioactive substances, and the tombs as a readily available opportunity to insert in them jars with mud, the ideal and available binder to hold the lethal product together and dilute its concentration to the desired degree.

SUMMARY

# THEY ALL DIED

Kings and paupers, men and beasts, fauna and flora, all died out in ancient Egypt. Modern science has given us the explanation for many of these unusual deaths: the presence of lethal radiation.

Although such a conclusion is hardly believable, given the semi-primitive level of the ancient Egyptian society, going back to at least 4,000 BC, we have to face the reality of the evidence, wherever it leads us. Facts and their scientific interpretation have to be the determining factors, when extracting a coherent meaning from the physical evidence in front of us.

If the discovered evidence is powerful enough to support the conclusion - no matter how unexpected it might be, or how farfetched it might appear, it would mean that we did not quite understand, nor properly analyze the difference between what history reported (mostly, as given to us by ancient sources), and what the physical facts are displaying. Many times, the latter did not fit in with ancient lore nor with the interpretation we had assigned to it. Such a dichotomy hints at the fact that although we learned quite a lot, seemingly it did not represent the full picture. There were covert realities and aspects that remained hidden behind the façade of the teaching of ordinary Egyptology. To paraphrase an old saying, realistic facts can be stranger than fiction!

The evidence strongly indicates that, given the symptoms displayed by at least Carnarvon, Mace, Breasted, Carter and Bouriant, these five archaeologists had died from radiation sickness.

Although many other individuals were referred to by various authors as possible victims of the "Curse", the lack of specificity offered preclude us from including them into the same category of irradiated persons. We simply do not have sufficient data given to us.

The conclusion that fatal radioactivity existed within Tutankhamun's tomb, is suggested by a number of other factual observations:

A- It has been established that this 3,200 year-old tomb had been entered into, sometime in antiquity most probably within a relatively short time after the burial. This became apparent as the intruders used one of Tutankhamun's old seals which they pressed against the wet plaster they had used to reseal the rebuilt walls, after having knocked down some sections so as to give them access to the rooms.

B- In the past, such reentries had been considered to have been performed by "thieves." Yet, the facts in the present case do not support such a conclusion. Thieves enter the premises of a tomb in order to steal gold or other valuables. They certainly do not go to the lengthy trouble of rebuilding walls, plastering and imprinting them in such a masterful manner that the site remains hidden for some 3,200 years. In addition, it is generally acknowledged that theft, *per se*, did not seem to have occurred, given the enormous treasures that were left in the rooms. In fact, there was hardly any space left in the chambers where additional artifacts could have been stored. One must conclude that theft of valuables—as is commonly understood, was not the purpose of the reentry.

C- Nevertheless, it was established that something was missing. The contents of dozens of emptied jars had been taken away after forcefully removing their sealing caps. The empty jars displayed, on their insides, a coating of some black, tar-like material, or an oily film of some resinous substance. Obviously, to the "thieves", the contents of those jars were much more precious than gold. When we analyze such an occurrence in light of our modern, scientific activities, we realize that tar-like materials, or gooey, resinous substances can be used as "binders" when mixed with radioactive products. In our present society, molten glass is being used, which, when mixed with radioactive waste, creates a block that is easier to handle and precludes loss of the lethal ingredients. In Tutankhamun's case, they had used tar or a resinous substance. However, in the great majority of other tombs excavated in Egypt, it was found that mud had been used as a binding agent, a substance in great abundance, easily and cheaply obtainable from the shores of the Nile.

D- The corpse of Tutankhamun displayed tell-tale aspects found in people exposed to radiation: (a) his hair had fallen off, and (b) he had burnt skin on a good part of his body.

E- As radioactivity existed in this underground tomb, it is most probable that other tombs were used to store similar lethal substances. The death of archaeologist Bouriant is a good example. He never entered Tutankhamun's tomb, but, nevertheless, he died of the same type of sickness that befell Carnarvon, Mace, Carter and Breasted.

If radioactive materials were being handled in ancient Egypt, there would likely have been fallout polluting the air, ground, and waters. As a consequence, men, animals, fish, and flora must have absorbed some lethal dosages, and, as a result, must have perished. In fact, archaeologists did discover enormous quantities of all sorts of animals, birds, fish, and crocodiles buried in the vast western Egyptian desert. This provides an understanding as to why a number of species of animals, fish, crocodiles, and flora disappeared from Eqypt. They became extinct, unable to reproduce healthy new generations of their kind. For example, crocodiles used to be plentiful in their habitat of Lower Egypt. They no longer exist there. Instead there are thousands of dead crocodiles in tombs and caves, miles away from the shores of the Nile, including their young ones and even their eggs and hatchlings! Likewise, ibises, baboons, and hippopotami have expired and no longer exist.

The discovery of the presence of radioactivity in ancient Egypt receives support from another mysterious aspect encountered in ancient underground tombs, the existence of fires and/or searing heat that permeated them. Up to now, we were confronted with lame explanations: supposedly, the perennial "thieves" had started fires in these underground tombs in order to cover up their misdeed, or else, because they were upset at not finding sufficient treasures to steal. Of course, such an alibi did not make any sense.

We now have the scientific explanation as to why there had to be intense heat and even fires within those underground tombs. Radioactive substances, besides being lethal, emit sustained waves of searing heat. Depending upon the quantities stored in a specific chamber, the result could be only an elevated temperature in the room (as was the case in Tutankhamun's premises), or it could translate itself into substantial amounts of heat waves that can consume the contents of the chamber involved.

We now have a cogent reason why substantial quantities of charcoal have been found in underground tombs. Charcoal is produced when wood is exposed to high degrees of temperature, but in the absence of oxygen, that is, air. As most of the tombs were, for all practical purposes, hermetically sealed, the heat generated did not encounter oxygen. Had air been abundantly available within those chambers, the wood would have been consumed by flames, in which case the residue would have been ashes, and not charcoal.

Also, as a result of the present discovery, we can now understand the reason for the condition of a number of tombs discovered by Petrie (and others). Black sun- dried bricks used in some of the underground tombs were found to have become red, fired bricks because of the intense heat to which they had been exposed. Petrie, while relating these observations described them as being "vitrified" and "calcified", terms that convey absorption of exceedingly elevated searing heat prevalent within those particular tombs.

In due time, when we study the policy of radioactive waste storage in ancient Egypt, we shall realize that they applied a different approach than we do in this country. In the United States, the Department of Energy (DOE), after years of intense studies, decided to concentrate all nuclear waste generated in this country in one site. They planned to create an underground storage facility in the Yucca Mountains of Nevada. This project has now been delayed because of the objections raised by some members of the scientific community. In ancient Egypt, however, they applied the exact opposite policy: instead of concentrating all radioactive materials in one spot, they dispersed them throughout the vast expanse of the western desert. Not only that, they diluted the lethal effect of the buried quantities by varying the concentration of the radioactive portion in the mixture with inert mud, tar, or other binding agents. There were thousands upon thousands of sites containing (or having contained) varying degrees of the dangerous product in question, thus greatly reducing the concentration of the toxicity levels buried in Egypt.

However, at this point we realize the existence of a different policy than the one applied by the US Government. While our authorities have been trying to create one permanent underground installation to bury said lethal substance, the picture we encounter in Egypt is different. While it is true that the organizers active in ancient Egypt did bury said dangerous material in thousands of different sites, what had not been realized till now is the fact that the same organizers were also the ones who re-entered the burial sites and retrieved most of the lethal jars. What happened thereafter will be submitted and described in a subsequent book of the present research study.

Because of this farsighted policy of the ancient organizers of 5000-6000 years ago, it is almost certain that, except for a few isolated instances, today's known desert sites and archaeological areas are probably no longer dangerous to human and animal lives. This would include all the areas visited by the tourists and/ or inhabited by locals. It should not be forgotten that the Egyptian Authorities are quite knowledgeable and capable to supervise newly and/or older discovered underground burials to ascertain that they would not constitute a danger.

When this newly-acquired knowledge is pursued and applied to other aspects of unsolved problems in Egypt's ancient history, we will discover a whole new dimension to the past of that country and of humanity.

The next step in the present research project is to determine who in the ancient Egyptian society was responsible for producing and handling radioactive substances. This question will be answered and fully described in a forthcoming book in this publication series.

STAY TUNED!

# EPILOGUE

This research has clarified four very important and enigmatic problems that had remained unsolved for centuries.

We started with the mysterious "Curse", which, when properly analyzed, turned out to have been radiation sickness — an unknown malady in the 1920s and 1930s. The five examples submitted clearly displayed the symptoms of that affliction.

The same solution also unraveled another age-old enigma of ancient Egypt. Why had birds, fish, and land animals died by the millions upon millions? We now understand the reason for the massive slaughter that took place at different times during the extended history of that ancient society.

In addition, we obtained the key to answering a third unsolved mystery that baffled us for a great many years: why were so many underground burial chambers burnt?

And, finally, we understood why Tutankhamun's mummy displayed a severely burnt face (and other areas).

The underlying solution to all four problems became clear: radioactivity. As a result, we can now also understand why ancient Egypt has been considered to be the land of death and burials.

When we look at an overview of the various aspects discovered by the present research project, as described in this book, we realize that we are facing two Egyptian societies. The frontal facade is well-known to all of us as described by archaeologists and Egyptologists. However, we also discovered that there was a completely different group of people performing activities in a covert manner and hiding them behind the well-known daily activities of ignorant people that populated Egypt in those years. It is an undeniable fact that ancient Egyptians, as we came to know them, did not have the knowledge, technical capacity, nor the available power to be able to create and manage those covert activities pertaining to radioactivity.

And yet, the facts speak for themselves.

There are some key requirements that have to be met when choosing a site to bury radioactive waste:

1- The rock formation has to be a stable one, which means it should not have geological faults, or fractures, and be known to be normally free from earthquakes and ground slides *(Note: just as in most of the rocky soil under the Egyptian desert, located a number of miles from the western bank of the Nile river. Some earthquakes do occur from time to time in certain parts of Egypt).*

2 - It should be a hard rock formation having a very low penetrability to water *(Note: just as found in parts of the subsoil of Egypt).*

3 - Granite and limestone are to be preferred since they constitute strong, dense crystalline rocks with chemical and structural stability, low penetrability, and good heat tolerance *(Note: just as was found in a good part of Egypt with its extensive geological formations of limestone)*

4 - It should not have any circulating groundwater *(Note: just as in Egypt, where the rocky soil under large areas of the desert is above ground water level.)*

5 - It should not be in the vicinity of populated areas, vegetation, or animal habitats *(Note: just as in Egypt, where large, sections of the desert areas were bare, not populated, and arid)*

6 - Even though no ground water is wanted, a steady ample supply is still needed—one that would not be contaminated by the radioactive waste deposited in the rocky subsoil. Water is essential for decontamination and the immersion of "hot" waste in basins or pools located next to the waste handling establishments *(Note: just like in ancient Egypt where the Nile provides*

*a constant stream of fresh water and where large pools or lakes had been constructed)*

7 - The area should be as dry as possible, having hardly any rainfall *(Note: just as in ancient Egypt where hardly any rain falls in most of the desert areas.)*

We observe that precautionary requirements modern mankind decided on for a safe waste disposal ambiance were to be found in the Egyptian landscape. The selection of Egypt for the creation of enormous pyramids, so-called temples, and a myriad of underground shafts, tunnels, passages, rooms, chambers, tombs was not an accidental or capricious choice. The organizers knew exactly what they needed and chose the type of geographical area that would meet most of the various requirements. Nevertheless, there is a probable difference. Their aim does not seem to have been to bury radioactive substances and leave them there. Through the findings of archaeologists, we realize that in a great many instances those lethal supplies had mostly been retrieved by them. We could perhaps realize that such a step might indicate a temporary warehousing necessity until they were ready to proceed with their subsequent activities, whatever these might have been.

There is another aspect that must be kept in mind. No new cases of the "Curse" seem to have been encountered, thus confirming that radioactivity is not likely to be present in any of the inhabited regions. This might be due to the ancient managers' policy of retrieving the buried quantities originally placed underground. However, there is another possible reason: the half-life of the elements they used to create the radioactive substances. For example, the element Americum 241 displays a half-life of only 458 years which, for all practical purposes would no longer be lethal today. There could be other elements that scientists of 5000 to 6000 years ago might have used—elements with shorter half-lives.

## Postscript

The research and writing of the present book was performed and finished during the past many years. It submits a number of new aspects that I discovered while studying the archaeology of ancient Egypt.

I am forced to add a postscript to my finished (but delayed) book because of an important event that took place in February 2014 – one that made the headlines of the papers and other various media.

The world learned that:

Since a number of years, the United States Department of Energy (DOE) has found and applied a method to bury radioactive waste that was "tame" and safe enough to be buried underground and would (ideally) stay peacefully there for centuries to come. Their procedure was to mix the radioactive waste with a type of cat litter, the principal component of which is clay.

However, in February 2014, a major radiation accident occurred in the Waste Isolation Pilot Project (WIPP). This facility in New Mexico is one of the largest DOE warehouses (underground or above ground) for high- and low-level nuclear waste[1,2]. For years, it had been the practice of the DOE to bury low-level radioactive "transuranic" waste in barrels to which had been added cat litter. Because the latter was primarily made of clay, it absorbed nitrates and other substances that occur in radioactive waste. In reality, it means that the US has been adding <u>mud</u> to its nuclear waste containers to stabilize them.

In February, 2014, a worker used a different type of cat litter that had not been made from clay (i.e., mud). Instead, they had used a "greener" type made from organic material such as leaves, wheat

---

1   http://www.npr.org/blogs/thetwo-way/2014/05/23/315279895/organic-kitty-litter-chief-suspect-in-nuclear-waste-accident

2   www.theverge.com/2014/5/23/5742800/did-kitty-litter-just-kill-the-most-success-ful-nuclear-waste-facility

or corn by-products. Rather than bind with the litter, the radioactive material began to heat up, ultimately resulting in an explosion that spread radiation within the facility and contaminated 22 workers. It is estimated that there are 500 barrels of this dangerous waste + organic cat litter mixture at WIPP and at Los Alamos, and in a temporary facility in Texas. The WIPP facility is now closed indefinitely until the DOE can determine how to process these containers and remove the organic cat litter. The quality of the mud additive thus explains which containers are stable and which generate heat.

When we compare what I discovered in ancient Egypt with today's activities for safe-keeping of nuclear waste by the DOE, we observe that most of the steps modern science has taken for the safe handling have direct parallels with their handling in ancient Egypt.

Underground burial: The DOE tries to bury this dangerous product in special underground installations and considers that it will be safe for thousands of years thereafter. The ancient Egyptians buried containers of treated radioactive waste underground (in "tombs");

Binder/stabilizer: DOE uses cat litter to bind the radioactive materials, whereas the ancient engineers arranged to reduce the degree of radioactivity by mixing it with plain mud (collected from the shores of the Nile) and other substances. These were placed in a sturdy stone container and left for a while to "cook" and solidify. Furthermore, the mixture they created consisted of, at least, the radioactive substance + mud + chopped down human / animal bones (rich in calcium, phosphorus, etc.). One of the methods currently being investigated by nuclear scientists is to encase intermediate and high-level radioactive materials in a calcium phosphate-based cement.[3,4]

Heat: The DOE worker's mistake in using organic material in the binder caused the barrel of waste to heat and explode. Likewise, tombs containing many container of the mud mixture (perhaps with straw or other organic materials) were found to have smoldered and burned.

These discoveries of radioactive materials and their handling in ancient Egypt and their relation to modern scientific practices cannot be mere coincidences but rather are the result of a pattern of observations and results that all add up to one thing – radiation was present and utilized throughout Egypt, and perhaps elsewhere in the ancient world. There is more to this story…

[3] Eric R. Vance and Daniel J. Gregg, Calcium phosphate materials for radioactive waste immobilization, *Calcium Phosphate: Structure, Synthesis, Properties, and Applications*, Chapter 18, Nova Science Publishers, Robert Heimann, editor, 2012, pp. 445-465.

[4]. Swift, P. Kinoshita, H. Collier, N. and Utton, C. (2013). Phosphate-modified calcium aluminate cement for radioactive waste encapsulation. *Advances in Applied Ceramics, 112(1),* pp. 1-8.

# ABBREVIATIONS

| | |
|---|---|
| ASAE: | Annales, Service Des Antiquites De L'Egypte |
| BIFAO: | Bulletin, Institut Francais d'Archeologie Orientale |
| BMMA: | Bulletin, Metropolitan Museum of Art, New York |
| BSAE: | British School of Archaeology in Egypt |
| CdE: | Chronique d'Egypte |
| EEF: | Egypt Exploration Fund |
| EES-TTS: | Egyptian Exploration Society—Theban Tombs Series |
| FIFAO: | Fouilles, Institut Francais d'Archeologie Orientale |
| JEA: | Journal of Egyptian Archaeology |
| KMT: | KMT Magazine |
| MDAIK: | Mitteilungen des Deutschen Arch. Institut, Abteilung Kairo |
| MEEF: | Memoirs, Egypt Exploration Fund |
| MMAEE: | Metropolitan Museum of Art—Egypt Expedition |
| OAW: | Osterreichische Akademie der Wissenschaften |
| OR: | Orientalia |
| RdE: | Revue d'Egyptologie |
| VDAIK: | Veroffentlichungen, Deutsche Arch.lnstitut -Abteilung Kairo |

# BIBLIOGRAPHY

| | | |
|---|---|---|
| ABOU SEIF, H | 1926 | Rapport sur les Fouilles faites a Tehneh (ASAE v 26) |
| ARNOLD, D | 1980 | Dahshur— Dritler Grabungsbericht (MDAIK v 36) |
| ARNOLD, D | 1982 | Die Pyramide Amenemhet III yon Dahshur (in MDAIK v 38) |
| ARNOLD, D | 1992 | Pyramid Complex of Senwosret I, v III |
| BAGNANI, G | 1952 | The Great Egyptian Crocodile Mystery(Archaeology 5) |
| BARSANTI, A | 1916 | La necropole des grands pretres d'Heliopolis sous l'Ancien Empire, Pt 2 (ASAE v16) |
| BELZONI, G | 1820 | Narrative of the Operations and recent discoveries in Egypt and Nubia |
| BENNETT, J | 1939 | The Restoration Inscription of Tutankhamun(JEA 25) |
| BRACKMAN, A C | 1976 | The Search for the Gold of Tutankhamen |
| BREASTED, C | 1923 | Over the Threshold of Tutankhamen's Tomb (ASIA23) |
| BRODINE, V | 1974 | Radioactive Contamination |
| BRUNTON, G | 1920 | Lahun I (BSAE v 27) |
| BRUNTON, G | 1939 | Howard Carter ( ASAE v 39) |
| BRUYERE, B | 1925 | Fouilles de Deir El Medineh (FIFAO v 2) |
| BRUYERE, B | 1934 | Les Fouilles de Deir El Medineh (FIFAO v10,sect 1) |
| CARTER, H | 1972 | The tomb of Tutankhamen |
| CARTER, H/MACE, A.C. | 1977 | The Discovery of Tutankhamun's Tomb |
| CHARRON, A | 1989 | Massacres d'Animaux a la Base Epoque (RdE v41) |
| CHASSINAT, E | 1903 | Necrologie (BIFAO v 3) |
| CHASSINAT, E | 1934 | Le temple de Dendera, v 3 |
| DARESSY, M G | 1905 | Statues de divinites v II |
| DARESSY, M.G | 1905A | Un Edifice Archaique a Nezlet Batran (ASAE v 6) |
| DARESSY, M.G | 1906 | Statues de divinites v I |

| | | |
|---|---|---|
| DAVIES, N de G | 1920 | The Tomb of Antefoker (EES-TTS v 2) |
| DAVIES, S | 2006 | The Mother of APIS and Baboon Catacombs |
| DAVIS, T.M. | 1912 | The Tombs of Harmhabi and Touatankhamanou |
| DeBONO, F | 1951 | Expedition Archeologique Royale au desert Oriental (ASAE v 51, 59-91) |
| DeGOROSTARZU, X | 1901 | Lettre sur deux Tombeaux de Crocodiles Decouverts au Fayoum (ASAE v 2, 182-184) |
| DERRY, D.E. | 1972 | Report upon the Examination of Tutankhamen's Mummy |
| DESROCHE-NOBLECOURT, C | 1963 | Life and Death of a Pharaoh: Tutankhamen |
| DODSON, A / IKRAM, S | 1998 | The Mummy in Ancient Egypt |
| DOLAN, E / SCARIANO, M | 1990 | Nuclear Waste-the 10,000 year Challenge |
| DORMAN, P | 1991 | The tombs of Harmhabi and Touatankhamanou |
| DZIOBEK, E | 1994 | Die Graber des Vezirs User-Amen,Theban No.61 und 131 (MDAIK v 84) |
| EATON-KRAUSS, M | 1993 | The Sarcophagus in the Tomb of Tutankhamun (in KMT 2010) |
| EATON-KRAUSS, M | 2010 | The Burial of Tutankhamen (KMTv21-1, p18-36) |
| EIGNER, D | 1983 | Das Thebanishe Grab des Amenhotep,Wesir von Unter Agypten: Die Architektur (MDAIK v 39) |
| EIGNER, D | 1984 | Die Monumentalen Grabbauten der Spatzeit in der Thebanischen Metropole (OAW v 6) |
| EMERY, W.B. | 1939 | 1$^{st}$ Dynasty Copper Treasures from N.Saqqara (ASAE v 39) |
| EMERY, W.B. | 1949 | Excavation at Saqqara v1 (Great Tombs of 1$^{st}$ Dynast) |

| EMERY, W.B. | 1954 | Excavation at Saqqara v2(Great Tombs of 1st Dynast) |
|---|---|---|
| EMERY, W.B. | 1958 | Excavation at Saqqara v3(Great Tombs of 1st Dynast) |
| EMERY, W.B. | 1966 | Prelim Report on the Excavations at Saqqara (JEA52) |
| EMERY, W.B. | 1969 | Prelim. Report on the Excavations at Saqqara (JEA55) |
| EMERY, W.B. | 1970 | Prelim.Report on the Excavations at Saqqara (JEA56) |
| EMERY, W.B. | 1971 | Prelim.Report on the Excavations at Saqqara (JEA57) |
| ENGLEBACH, R | 1938A | A hitherto unknown Statue of King Tutankhamun |
| FAKHRY, A | 1959 | The Monuments of Snefru at Dahshur v 1 |
| FIRTH, C.M. | 1928 | Excavations at Saqqara (ASAE v28) |
| FIRTH, C.M. | 1929 | Excavations at Saqqara (ASAE v29) |
| GAIN, E. | 1902 | Etudes sur les Bles de Momie (ASAE v 3) |
| GERA, F. | 1981 | Geologic Predictions and Radioactive Waste Disposal (in Productive Geology, Pergamon Press) |
| GERSHEY, E et al | 1990 | Low level Radioactive Waste |
| GINSBURG, L | 1999 | Les Chats Momifies du Bubasteon de Saqqarah (ASAE v 51,74) |
| GOLVIN, J-C | 1987 | Les Batisseurs de Karnak |
| GONEIM, Z. | 1957 | Excavations at Saqqara-Horus Sekhemkhet |
| GOUDSMIT, J. / BRANDON-JONES, D | 1999 | Mummies of Olive Baboons and Barbary MAcaques in "The Baboon Catacomb of the Sacred Animal Necropolis at North Saqqara" (JEA 85, 45-53) |
| GRIMAL, N,et al | 2006 | Fouillies et Travaux en Egypte et Soudan (OR 75/3) |
| HABACHI, L | 1956 | Mit Rahineh |
| HARARI, I | 1951 | Bernard Grdseloff (ASAE v 51 ,p123) |

| | | |
|---|---|---|
| HOLLICK, M.F. | 1996 | Vitamin D and bone Health (Journal of Nutrition 126) |
| HORNBOSTEL C | 1978 | Construction Materials |
| HOVING, T | 1978 | Tutankhamun, the untold story |
| IKRAM, S. | 2005 | Divine Creatures |
| IKRAM, S. | 2006 | Nile Currents (KMT v 18-1) |
| IKRAM, S. | 2008 | Nile Currents (KMT v 19-3) |
| IKRAM, S. | 2010 | Nile Currents (KMT v 21-1) |
| JAMES, T.G.H. | 1972 | The Archaeology of Ancient Egypt |
| JAMES, T.G.H. | 1992 | Howard Carter |
| KESSLER, D. | 1987 | Tuna El Gebel- Die Tiergalerien |
| KESSLER, D. | 1989 | Die Heiligen Tieren und der Konig |
| LEBLANC, C. | 1983 | Les Tombes NO.58 et NO.60 de la Vallee des Reines (ASAE v 69) |
| LECA, A.P. | 1981 | The Egyptian Way of Death |
| LECLANT, J | 1966 | Fouilles et Travaux en Egypte et auSoudan (OR v 35) |
| LECLANT, J | 1967 | Fouilles et Travaux en Egypte et auSoudan (OR v 36) |
| LECLANT, J | 1992 | Fouilles et Travaux en Egypte et au Soudan (OR v61) |
| LECLANT, J/CLERC, G | 1997 | Fouilles et Travaux en Egypte et au Soudan (OR 66) |
| LEE, C.C. | 1992 | Arthur C. Mace |
| LIPSCHUTZ, R.D | 1980 | Radioactive Waste: Politics, Technology, and Risk |
| LOAT, W.L. | 1905 | Gurob (8SAE v 10) |
| LOAT, W.L. | 1914 | The Ibis Cemetery at Abydos ( JEA v 1) |
| LORTET, L | 1905 | Les Momies animals de l''Ancienne Egypte (Revue des deux Mondes, tome 27, p368-390) |
| LORTET/GAILLARD, C | 1902 | Sur les Oiseaux Momifies (ASAE v 3) |
| LORTET/GAILLARD, C | 1909 | La Faune Momifiee de l''Ancienne Egypte |
| MANNING, S | 1875 | The Land of the Pharaohs |
| MARIETTE, A | 1870 | Denderah 3 v |

| MARIETTE, A | 1871 | Denderah v III |
|---|---|---|
| MARIETTE, A | 1882 | Le Serapeum de Memphis |
| McQUITTY, W | 1976 | Island of Isis |
| MENDELSSOHN, K | 1974 | The Riddle of the Pyramids |
| MERRITT, F /LOFTIN, M / RICKETTS, J | 1996 | Standard Handbook for Civil Engineers |
| MINAULT-GOUT, A | 1983 | Rapport Preliminaire sur la Quatrieme Campagne de Fouille du Mastaba II a 8alat: Neuf Tombes du Secteur Nord (ASAE v 69) |
| MINAULT-GOUT, A | 1992 | 8alat II-Le Mastaba d'ima-Pepi (Mastaba III) |
| MURRAY, M/LOAT, WL | 1905 | Saqqara Mastabas I and Gorub (8SAE v 10) |
| NAVILLE, E | 1891 | Bubastis (MEEF v 8) |
| NICHOLSON, P | 1994 | Prelim.report on Work at the Sacred Animal Necropo- lis N.Saqqara 1992 (JEA v 80) |
| NICHOLSON, P. | 1995 | The Sacred Animal Necropolis at N.Saqqara (JEA 81) |
| PEAKE, F.T. | 1930 | An Adventure in the Crocodile Caves of Maabdeh (Ancient Egypt v 14) |
| PEET, E | 1914 | The Cemeteries of Abydos Pt II (MEEF v 34) |
| PEET, E/LOAT, WL | 1913 | The Cemeteries of Abydos Pt 2 (Memoirs MEEF v 35) |
| PETRIE, F | 1930 | Anteopolis -the tombs of Qau (8SAE v 51) |
| PETRIE, F | 1890 | Kahun,Gurob and Hawara |
| PETRIE, F | 1900 | The Catacombs of Sacred Animals(MEEF v 17,28-30) |
| PETRIE, F | 1900A | The Royal Tombs of the First Dynasty (in Memoirs of EEF v 21) |
| PETRIE, F | 1901 | Diospolis Parva (MEEF v 20) |
| PETRIE, F | 1901A | The Royal Tombs of the Earliest Dynasties Pt II |
| PETRIE, F | 1907 | Gizeh and Rifeh (BSAE v 13) |

| PETRIE, F | 1912 | The Labyrinth Gerzeh and Mazghuneh ( BSAE v 21) |
| PETTIGREW, T.J | 1834 | A History of Egyptian Mummies |
| POCKOCKE, R | 1814 | Travels in Egypt (Pinkerton-Voyages and Travels v15) |
| PRINGLE, L.P. | 1989 | Nuclear Energy |
| RAY, J.D. | 1978 | The World of N. Saqqara (World Archaeology, Oct1978) |
| REEVES, C.N. | 1990 | Valley of the Kings: The Decline of a Royal Necropolis |
| REEVES, C.H. | 1990 | Valley of the Kings |
| REISNER, G | 1931 | Mycerinus |
| RHIND, A.H. | 1862 | Thebes, Its Tombs and Their Tenants |
| ROUYER, P.C. | 1809 | Notice sur les Embaumements des Anciens Egyp- tiens (Antiquites, Memoires v VII,p 207-220) |
| ROWE, A | 1931 | Excavations at Meydum (1929-30) |
| ROXBURGH, I.S | 1987 | Geology of High-level Nuclear Waste Disposal |
| SAYCE, A/CLARKE, S | 1905 | Report on certain Excavations made at El-Kab during the years 1901-04 (ASAE v 6) |
| SEIF, H.A. | 1926 | Rapport sur les Fouilles Faites a Tehneh (ASAE v 26) |
| TIERNEY, L/McPHEE, S | 2001 | Current Medical Diagnosis and Treatment |
| VANDENBERG, P | 1975 | The Curse of the Pharaohs |
| WAINWRIGHT, G | 1910 | Meydun and Memphis III (BSAE v 18) |
| WAINWRIGHT, J.M | 1852 | The Land of Bondage |
| WHITIEMORE, T | 1914 | The Ibis Cemetery at Abydos (JEA v 1) |
| WILKINSON, J,G | 1841 | Manners and Customs of the Ancient Egyptians |
| WINLOCK, H.E | 1942 | Excavations at Deir El Bahri (1923-24) |
| WINSTONE, H.V.F. | 1986 | Uncovering the Ancient World (Facts on File, p 119) |

# ILLUSTRATION & PHOTO CREDITS

Fig. 1: ©New Research, LLC; Fig. 2: Harry Burton (Griffith Institute, University of Oxford); Fig. 3: Chicago Daily News; Fig. 4: R.G. Harrison; Fig. 5: ©New Research, LLC; Fig. 6: Eric Hooymans; Fig. 7:Bjorn Christian Torrissen; Fig 8: Jean-Pierre Dalbera; Fig. 10: Thames & Hudson Co.; Fig. 11: Smudger888; Fig. 12: Liz Roy; Fig. 13: Jnissa; Fig. 14: Terry Foote; Fig. 15: Peet (1914); Fig. 16: Yathinsk; Fig. 17: Mariette (1870A); Fig. 18: Mariette (1871); Fig. 19-21: Egypt Exploration Society; Fig. 22: Brunton (1920); Fig. 23: Dodson (1998); Fig. 24: Bruyere (1934); Fig. 25: Davis (1912); Fig. 26: Davis (1912); Fig. 27: Eigner (1984). Back-cover crocodile: Marco Schmidt

www.ingramcontent.com/pod-product-compliance
Lightning Source LLC
Chambersburg PA
CBHW071956090426
42740CB00011B/1962